What (

MW00529661

I have known Marcia for over twenty-four years. I first met her when she became a newspaper reporter during my sixteen-year tenure as mayor of Bellbrook. Her written word has always sparked people's interest and curiosity, no matter the subject. When I first met her, I knew she was special.

—Mary C. Graves, Bellbrook, Ohio, Retired Mayor

Transcending the Heart is an enthusiastic celebration of the history of the small town of Bellbrook and Sugarcreek Township, Ohio. Marcia J. Treadway offers a unique tribute to its early settlers and vaporous visitors. She thrives on the feeling of community that is created when people know and respect each other.

While the emphasis of her work is extremely personal, it contains much that will be of interest to those fascinated with the history and folklore of a small town. The author has selected several ghostly and spiritual experiences as key subjects, although these represent only a small sample of the activity documented in Bellbrook.

This book is designed to play a major role in educating the next generation on small-town history, investigation, God, and one's personal spirituality.

—David Jones, Lebanon, Ohio,
Information security analyst,
Paranormal researcher of more than
fifteen years

Friendship must have a foundation of trust. Working with Marcia J. Treadway cemented that foundation, as she regards everyone's point of view with compassion and seriousness. You will experience that in this book.

Transcending the Heart is a must-read from the beginning to the end. You will encounter an "edge of your seat" adventure, profound sadness, and mystical enlightenment, bundled with a touch of humor.

Since the first day I met Marcia, she demonstrated a level of integrity and professionalism that set her apart from many other individuals I have worked with. She has tenacious willpower when it comes to her passions that has often allowed her to open doors that many would never have been able to access. I believe all these strong qualities will continue to lead her down a bright path, no matter what she sets out to accomplish.

There is so much I admire about Marcia, and I think her raw honesty may be the best part. She is a good friend whom I will always trust.

—Johnathan C. Brown, Cincinnati, Ohio
United States Air Force veteran, electrical and computer engineering technician, Clinical engineering biomedical technician, Parapsychology and paranormal researcher of more than ten years

When Marcia J. Treadway writes, I read. She doesn't write for a living; she lives to write. For her it's all about the message, and her message in *Transcending the Heart* has a reverent meaning for all. I love God, I love adventure, and I love this book.

—Laura Martin, New Carlisle, Ohio
Copilot, wing walker, parachutist,
base jumper, and bungee jumper

Marcia Treadway is one of the best newspaper reporters our community ever had. She is an unassuming, "behind the scenes" kind of person whose first loyalty in her work has always been to the citizens of Sugarcreek Township and Bellbrook. She is a woman with strong ethics; her writing is always backed up with facts, logic, and reason. She has the courage to go out on a limb to get her story, in pursuit of journalistic truth.

Since her retirement we have remained friends. We have lunch every Wednesday while discussing community affairs. I'll endorse Marcia 100 percent in anything she does . . . always.

—Jim "Pee Wee" Martin, Sugarcreek Township, Ohio
United States Army paratrooper / 101st Airborne Div. /
506th PIR / 3rd Battalion/G Company, World War II

TRANSCENDING THE HEART

When God Sent Me the Ghosts

A memoir by
Marcia J. Treadway

Transcending the Heart: When God Sent Me the Ghosts

Published by Wheatmark®
2030 East Speedway Boulevard, Suite 106
Tucson, Arizona 85719 USA
www.wheatmark.com

ISBN: 978-1-62787-964-4 (paperback)
ISBN: 978-1-62787-965-1 (ebook)
LCCN: 2022908997

Bulk ordering discounts are available through Wheatmark, Inc.
For more information, email orders@wheatmark.com
or call 1-888-934-0888.

Daniel sketch by Adryanne Cortes.

Disclaimer

This book is a memoir. It reflects the author's recollections of experiences over time as truthfully as an over sixty-year-old brain can recall and/or be verified by her evidence and research. All persons within are actual individuals; however, some names have been changed to respect their privacy. The information provided in this book is not intended to be a source of advice or encouragement to engage in any activities with respect to the material presented.

If you or someone you know is in crisis, help is available 24/7 by calling the National Suicide Prevention Lifeline at 1-800-273-TALK (8255).

You may also consider reaching out to the leader of a local religious faith community when faced with traumatic issues.

To my son, Daniel,
who walks where I have only wandered.

Sketch by Adryanne Cortes

Contents

Chance Encounter

Curious Connections

Yes, It Is True

Acknowledgments

Writing a book is a daunting task. It can take years off your life because it can take years to complete. I thought it appropriate to first thank my loving husband, Bob, who must have the patience of a saint to put up with the constant undone laundry and disorderly house, but then I remembered his way of life when I met him over thirty-seven years ago. His style was what I'd call "minimalist garage sale." His bedroom furniture consisted of a mattress on the floor with a wooden orange crate as a nightstand. He was the perfect mate for someone who would end up on a computer the majority of the day! I would like to extend my gratitude to Bob for his tolerance and for consistently reading my manuscript for clarity, from which several profoundly intimate conversations emerged.

I am also grateful to my family members who supported me during this endeavor, especially my daughter, Jennifer, and grandchildren—Carly, Austin, Brittney, Alyssa, and Courtney. I am amazed I was able to master writing with a four-year-old sitting by my side.

I'm deeply indebted to those who shared their skills

and gifted me their time to make my book the best it could be. Thanks to Sharon Oldham, who professionally proofread and edited my book; to Susan Lopez, who helped me through a rather difficult chapter; and to Nadine Daugherty, my test reader. Many thanks go to Deborah Staton, for her expertise in genealogy and continued support over the past decade.

I would like to recognize the assistance of Dave Jones and John Brown, who were instrumental in the development of my investigation skills and technical knowledge. Their insight and profound belief in my work are very much appreciated.

Particularly helpful were Chris Ewing, Lisa Greenwood, and Laura Martin. One kept me grounded, one kept me mystified, and the other opened my eyes to adventure.

I am forever grateful to Jennifer Hoehn for her constant support and our "long" conversations.

Special thanks go posthumously to my son, Danny; Jo Ann Brown; Carl Elliott; Rosemary Ellen Guiley; Ed Leen; Ann Litle; Mike Sabin; Wanda Kay Stephenson; Jonathan Winters; and William Wright, for their kindness, encouragement, or concern during this journey.

My love of life exists in my soul, and I would like to extend my sincere thanks to God and the priests who helped me complete my journey.

Finally, thanks to all those who have been a part of my getting to where I needed to be. Some are dear friends, and some are at most acquaintances. Each and every one of you has touched my life in a positive way. A partial list of those whom I am so grateful for: Angela Abraham, Lee and Patti Allen, Sandra Baer, Bill Baglio, Eric Baldino, Gina Barnes, Vickie Barnhill, Dwight Bartlett, Betsy Schrand Beech, Laurel Benner, Andrew Berryhill, Dave and Jan Berryhill, Stephen Berryhill, Kathy Bowermaster, Suzi Bowers, Amanda Braydich, Amy Perry-Brock, Kimberly Brouillette, Ericka Howell Captain, Taryn Carlson, Judy Carr, Eric Conner, Joedy Cook, Richard Cost, Cindi Crew, Eric Creyts, Debbi Custer, Jessica DAngelo, Cody Dalton, Brian and Darlene Danhausen, Greg Dart, Jay Day, Kristina Defibaugh, Patrick DeHart, Doug Doherty, Sheryl Dupree, Mark Eaton, Anji Erickson, Jessie Eubank, Kristen Everman, J.R. Ewing, Cheryl Fahrenholz, Andrea Fauber, Barbara Felder, Meg Fischer, Ron and Lyric Folkerth, Beth Fontaine, Garry Fox, Rodney Frisby, Jim and Carol Froehlich, Misty Garcia, Shari Geis, Kristin Ginett, Andi Lloyd Girard, Jann Goldberg, Mary Graves, Jon Greene, Jackie Greenwood, Heather Hansen, Mike and Stephanie Hartman, Yuvonna Hawkins, Angie Seifert Hayden, Mel Hayden, April Hayes, Amber Hess, Mike and Stephanie Hornback, Darin Hough, David Howard, Kristen Hutson, Hilary Johnson, Mike Johnson, Martin Jordan, Gail Kelly, Kelli Koch, Kim Kost, Austin Kunz, Kat Lang, Deb Lantz, Nick Lantz, Susan Eklund-Leen, Amanda Leetch, Kim Moore Leetch, Emilia Luce, Linda Madaffer, Cynthia Manz, Jason Manz, Dave and Mary Margerum, Jim Martin, Jodi Martin, Chris Matheny, David Miller, Shelly Moore, Krista Moser, Kate Nadaskay, Donna Nelson, Richard Palmisano, Andy Newell, Becky Partan, Brian Parthemore,

Victor Paruta, Eric and Monica Patrie, Laura Manz Middleton Phillips, Lisa Phillips, Tammy Phillipson, Jaiden Pridemore, Mark Possert, Kathy Proctor, Ben Rader, Denise Rector, Greta Refert, Lori Roberts, David Rountree, Cam Russell, Kate Says, Kelly Schley, Mark Schweikert, Daniel Serey, Jack Sexton, Alyssa Shockley, Brittney Shockley, Courtney Shockley, David Shockley, Jennifer Shockley, Kathleen Shockley, Mike Smith, Carly Spradlin, David Spradlin, Keith St.Pierre, Kristen Stamm, Janis Stratis, Caitlyn Suber, Danny Sullivan, Nancy Sumner, Valerie Sumpter, Teresa Tarter, Janice Tavalero, John Tenney, Kurma Thompson, Narayan Thompson, Shannon Thompson, Jenny Thorn, Taylor Thullen, Barry Tiffany (and sister Brenda), Debbie and Larry Tomlin, David Treadway, Janet Treadway, Robert Treadway, Sophia Treadway, Tracy Treadway, Katherine (Kitty) Ullmer, Vida VandeSlunt, Judy VanKuiken, Jeremy Wages, Christina Weaver, Ron Weaver, Ryan Weaver, Darrell Whisman, Connie Williams, Jamie Wilson, Jim Wilson, Peter Wixted, Sheila Woody, Cathy Young, and Takeshi Yukai.

It is because of all of you that I have this legacy to pass on.

From the Author

Fear of the paranormal is real. Phasmophobia is basically a fear of ghosts. The mere mention of the word "paranormal" can be enough to evoke irrational fear in many. For those people this phobia can be life limiting. Others, while enjoying the thrill of the adrenaline rush when hearing a ghost story or watching a scary movie, are able to control their temporary fear.

Then there are those who identify as skeptics and/or nonbelievers, who give the expected eye roll when "that" word (paranormal) is brought up.

Paranormal is constantly lumped together with horror. The horror genre wants to horrify you. The paranormal genre is considered fiction. My stories do not fit into either.

Humans can find it challenging to unlearn fears and lifelong beliefs. It is not my intention to try to prove or disprove anything to anyone with this book. I don't want to cause any tension or discomfort; so I decided, moving forward, to use the word "transnormal," instead of "paranormal," to better categorize my investigation and research.

While searching for a more neutral literary description,

I found that there were over forty synonyms for the word "paranormal" and over one hundred for "supernatural." Both words cross-referenced each other and shared many others, such as mystical, unearthly, superhuman, ghostly, occult, miraculous, etc. Knowing such things are not classified as "normal," I added the prefix "trans" in the internet search box, and there it was: "transnormal—beyond what is normal." There are no synonyms for the word and only one antonym: normal. It is associated with an obscure mathematics expression. (Feel free to look it up!)

I will reappropriate the word as a perfect description of my explorations. To avoid confusion for my readers, the word "paranormal" will remain in this book. As a writer I try not to fence my readers into a particular reaction or emotion. If you feel that way, it is my hope that you jump the fence and escape the confines into the larger realm of empathy, understanding, love, and "other" perspectives.

Preface

Not being what some would call an "open book," I admit that my life has not always been easy, and I've had to work hard at it. Over the years I've begun to realize that most people hide what isn't perfect in their lives, and nobody ever truly lives an idealistic life. Even those precious few people I've deemed to be flawless have, in fact, lived quite imperfect lives. I've written hundreds of articles for a national newspaper—both regional news and features about local people telling their personal stories and achievements. I am an accomplished writer in that arena; however, I never had the courage to tell any of my own stories . . . until now.

I was born in the mid-1950s and grew up in the 1960s and '70s. My family life experiences were full of tragic and dramatic occurrences (just about anything you might see in a made-for-TV movie). Premature, ill-timed, disease-ridden, and self-destructive deaths and suicides ravaged me off and on throughout my adult life. The majority of my loved ones died before they should have.

I don't fear the idea of death. I don't deny death. I know death is an inevitable part of life. What I don't like are "dead things." I cringe when I find a dead mouse or have to walk by a deceased animal when on a walk. I'm not necrophobic; I enjoy walking through cemeteries and admire the old and ornate tombstones. I am not afraid of coffins, although I am claustrophobic; however, as luck would have it (or not), *I* was always the one having to view and identify the bodies of my loved ones. Maybe I feel the way I do because I've had enough of it already.

I went through a period in my life during which I avoided funerals when I could. I didn't want to gaze upon a lifeless body missing its soul. I understood that funerals are for the living and have a number of therapeutic benefits for the immediate family and close friends. If a friend told me it was not necessary to attend a funeral of their relative, I took them at their word. My own mother insisted on private graveside services only. But slowly I came to the realization that my presence, even having only a few moments to express my condolences, spoke volumes to my friend or relative who was preparing to begin the long journey of grief.

At this juncture I hoped that the death of my loved ones had led them to liberation from their suffering, and if so, I wanted to celebrate it. But before I could celebrate, I wanted to know if it was true. I wanted to know if the afterlife really existed. Not being much of a religious person (at that time), I wondered how one went about finding out such a thing. When I searched "What does the Bible say about the afterlife?" on the internet, over fifty Bible verses appeared. While some verses mentioned eternal life, paradise, or that a place has been prepared for us, there were also the words "eternal punishment" and "second death," as well as phrases saying that the dead know nothing and have no more reward, etc. My family did not practice any type of Christian education, so these verses were not well defined or easy for me to understand.

I felt that the idea of an afterlife was not just a religious concept, and I decided that I was going to have to go looking into it myself. My goal now was not to immortalize my loved ones but to try to communicate with them in my heart and, if possible, in the hereafter. This journey of mine was unique. If you want to call it a spiritual journey, well, I did it backward. I didn't start out seeking God; I began looking for ghosts. Almost a decade later, after searching for answers through ghost-hunting experiences, was when I felt that God sought me. I spent years writing other people's stories. After a journey of investigation and discovery that transcended my heart, it is time I tell mine, now that God sent me the ghosts.

Marcia J. Treadway
Washington Township, Ohio

INTRODUCTION

The Spirited Little Town

Among the dense forests and pristine foothills on the land located east of the Little Miami River, where the spring-fed magnetic waters flow, the Shawnee, Miami, and Wyandot Native American tribes hunted bear, deer, rabbit, and buffalo in 1775. The unspoiled area was shrouded in shade from the thick woodlands of maple, birch, walnut, and oak. Even in daylight, the darkness wrapped around the forest like velvet, giving it a peculiar, spooky guise. This area, dubbed the Dark and Bloody Ground, set the stage for decades of ghost stories, haunting legends, and tales of the soul.

During this time a young Shawnee brave with the given name of Tecumseh was born in March 1768. He lived northeast, in the area now known as Xenia, in Greene County, Ohio. It was not yet known that this spirited Shawnee lad would frequent this area, become chief of the Shawnee, and lead a large tribal byand (known as Tecumseh's Confederacy) in warfare against the United States.

Tecumseh and his confederacy traveled northwest, allying with the British in the colonies of Upper Canada during the war of 1812. There he was brutally killed by American forces in the Battle of Thames. It is believed that Tecumseh's Great Spirit returned and still dwells on this land of bountiful resources.

The issuance of war bounty land grants—land issued by the government as a reward for hardships endured during military service—to soldiers who fought in the Revolutionary War gave incentive for families in search of their wondrous dream to become landowners to move. These brave pioneers had to survive the tedious journey west before facing the challenges of living in a new land, possibly encountering their former enemies.

The first settlers, taking notice of southwestern Ohio's vast, valuable resources, decided to call this vicinity home in 1796. Land could be purchased for $2 per acre, compared to $14 to $20 in the east, from whence they came. With the strength that God gave them, the settlers began the many long months of claiming and clearing the Dark and Bloody Ground.

In 1797, Joseph C. Vance Sr. built the first log cabin on the hill among the stunning sugar maple trees on the southeast corner of what is today Walnut and Main Streets in Bellbrook, Ohio. Because of its later use, this building would eventually be named a historic site.

Around 1802, Vance sold the rustic cabin to James Clancy (also written in the record as "Clancey" and "Clency"), who added on and used it as a large kitchen for his new two-story log building, which became known as Clancy's Tavern. Upon the county's organization into townships, this building was selected as the place to hold elections. Clancy's Tavern was used as a courtroom, a place for uplifting social gatherings, a preaching venue, and an inn for weary travelers.

With many meandering waterways suitable for sustaining grist- and sawmills, it wasn't long before other settlers arrived, including two prominent men: Stephen Bell and Henry Opdyke (also written in the record as "Updyke"). Bell, Opdyke, and Clancy, now known as the founding fathers of Bellbrook, platted the village in 1815, with eighty-four lots surveyed. In discussions over what to name the village, possibilities included Clancyville or Opdykeville. In February 1816, the official notice named the village Bellbrook—"Bell" after the last name of Stephen Bell and "brook" because of the small streams, brooks, and rivulets that ran through the foothills.

Bellbrook, now a bustling small town with the nearest mill about a mile away as the crow flies, housed 189 people comprising thirty-three families, according to the 1830 census. As the village grew, people of many occupations came to work here. Farmers, millers for gristmills and sawyers for sawmills, blacksmiths, livery hands, carpenters, and cabinetmakers (who also constructed coffins) made Bellbrook a well-rounded community.

To be wealthy in the 1800s, one had to own land. Grist- and sawmill owners were men of property, considered among the wealthiest residents of their respective districts. Looming legends of two millers whose lives came to abrupt ends in the midst of robbery and bloodshed on the land near Little Sugarcreek (once called Possum Run) documented a shocking world of crime in the sleepy little village of Bellbrook. The stories contain graphic accounts of horrific murder, and the men's ghosts supposedly lurk in the area of Little Sugarcreek, near where their mills once stood.

Little Sugarcreek is also ablaze with a heartbreaking tale of suicide. A married elected official had a mistress, who became pregnant. After her baby was born, the child looked so much like the official that he ordered the woman to keep the baby covered at all times. The mistress, destitute, crossed the bridge over Little Sugarcreek and knocked on the door of the man's house, begging for assistance. He turned her and the child away, and as the woman left, it is said that she jumped into the rushing water with her infant. The body of the woman, still holding the baby's blanket, washed up on shore. The infant was never found. This occurred in June, and the tale goes that during that month you can see the woman along Little Sugarcreek rocking and singing to her baby.

In the coming era, considerable acreage was given to corn, wheat, and tobacco; however, sugar production and pork packing also played important roles in the early life of the area.

Each autumn the view down the hill into the new village of Bellbrook was a sensational sight, as the sugar maple trees were clad in glorious, brilliant colors of scarlet, orange, and yellow. Main Street was lined with these grand trees, remarkable for their immense spread. The sugar maple trees in abundance every March were tapped with sap buckets hanging from their sides, allowing Bellbrook to become a marketing center for sugar products. In the early to mid-1800s, the farmers of Sugarcreek Township annually stirred off 24,524 pounds of maple sugar and 1,457 gallons of maple molasses. These products were hauled from Bellbrook to Cincinnati.

While Main Street produced such a beautiful sight, the crossroad of Franklin Street provided a grotesque scene, more in the way of a holocaust. Located in the midst of the village, an extensive pork packing business christened Bellbrook a "Porkopolis" and the business center of the territory. In 1835, a brick pork house was built at 22 East Franklin Street by Benjamin F. Allen, on the lot at which the former Township House now stands. The hog house and slaughterhouse were located up a small hill west of the village. The slaughterhouse processed 250 hogs each working day. Here the animals met their fates at the hands of the workers. A river of blood flowed just below the pen, into a small well that drained into the fertile ground. They were hauled in long processions of farmers' wagons piled high with the clean, white corpses, noses ornamented with blood-red icicles, and the round, red wounds adorning their foreheads showing where the final blow with the hammer had struck them down. The wagons going back and forth from slaughterhouse to pork house could be seen and heard all day . . . and sometimes well into the night. Delivery to the pork house resulted in weighing each cadaver, while workers with their huge, flying cleavers would begin the disassembly into hams, shoulders, and sides with relentless efficiency.

It is said that angels provide us with assistance and inspiration. When angels are at work around us, their divine energy helps increase our level of compassion and, in a "pay it forward" kind of way, give us guidance to help others, to make this world a better place.

In 1841, the inhabitants of Bellbrook witnessed a heavenly phenomenon, documented by the handwritten note of one of the daughters of Bellbrook founding father James Clancy. Mrs. Martha Ellis describes seeing many angels appearing in all of their heavenly glory. What the villagers saw in August 1841 were thought to have been the celestial messengers of God, allowing more angels to descend to earth. She wrote,

> I will mention one more strange phenomena [sic] that I witnessed in Bellbrook, August 19, 1841. We were viewing what, to us, was an unusual sight in the shape of an unusual band, when we noticed excited families of the neighborhood in the streets viewing the southeastern sky. A glance in that direction showed a phenomenon which consisted of angel forms in solemn procession, marching with stately tred [sic], through the realms of space in full view. In the heavens, marching by twos was a parade of what appeared to be human forms clad in flowing

robes. As fast as one company consisting of 10 to 15 couples would disappear from view, another would take its place. And the vision lasted ten minutes. The forms were so lifelike that seemingly the movements of the limbs could be distinguished. The people at that time were greatly excited about the angelic visitation, and in several instances families carried invalids out of doors that they might view the scene. The occurrence took place between 9 and 10 o-clock in the evening. The forms of the spirit visitors were to all appearances covered by a gauzy substance and their existence in companies was visible to the eye through a space of probably 30 degrees in a northwest direction.

In 1883, the discovery of a magical spring in the heart of Bellbrook brought thousands of people to the small village. The spring, more magnetic than magical, was discovered by accident after Andrew Byrd purchased the old United Presbyterian Church at the corner of Main and Walnut streets. It was his intention to convert the church building into apartments. Byrd began to dig a well in the basement of the house, but at a depth of only a few feet encountered such a strong vein of water that the digging was stopped. Soon after, Byrd hired Robert Butler to begin plastering. Butler used the water from the shallow well to mix mortar and soak his tools overnight. Upon his return the next day, he was amazed that his trowel had become magnetized. After some experimenting it was found that any piece of steel allowed to remain in the water from this well for a short time would attain magnetic qualities.

Byrd immediately thought that these spring waters might be credited with healing powers and had a sample analyzed by chemists. Soon dubbed the "Magnetic Springs," this "Fountain of Youth" quickly became a sensation, thanks to word of mouth. Citizens flocked to the healing waters to drink and bathe.

Over two hundred years of history, myth, and storytelling have contributed to a rich collection of legend and lore designating Bellbrook as Ohio's own "Sleepy Hollow." Or are the spooky myths and legends of years gone by based on true stories?

In the mid- to late 1800s, as the population of the United States doubled and the number of newspapers quadrupled, the small village of Bellbrook was having a hard time sustaining a profitable newspaper business. A tall, thin man with a long, pointy nose, Ole' Fiddler—editor and reporter of the *Bellbrook Moon* newspaper, who thought that he knew everything about anything—may have devised a way to sell more newspapers. It is believed that Ole' Fiddler enhanced (or even made up) stories about local ghostly phenomena and printed them in the *Bellbrook Moon* to increase sales. After all, ghost stories have been around as long as there have been stories themselves.

Notes

1. Bellbrook Historical Society, *Bellbrook 1816–1981*.
2. Marie-Ange Faugerolas, *Angels: The Definitive Guide to Angels from Around the World*.
3. George F. Robinson, *Robinson's History of Greene County*.
4. Alice Wiseman, Stephen Berryhill & George Simmons, *Bellbrook's First 100 Years*.

BEYOND FEAR

ONE

Non Compos Mentis

The book was finished, with the exception of one last chapter. "This shouldn't take long," I said to myself as I sat down at the computer. But I stared at the monitor, my expression blank. Where normally a creative downpour of ideas would flow came nothing. My brain battered my thoughts, yet my fingers remained still on the keyboard . . . until I thought about Lilly, my most frightening paranormal investigation of all time.

In June 2019, my friend Lisa, a former client turned investigator, and I arrived at the home of ninety-year-old Lillian promptly at seven o'clock, the agreed time of arrival. Lillian (Lilly) had contacted the historical museum in Bellbrook, Ohio, asking for help from a ghost hunter, and one of the museum trustees passed her phone number to me. A phone interview revealed she had a ghost in her basement that stole things and replaced them with items she did not want. She explained she lived in a town nearby and called the museum because she had read how haunted Bellbrook was. The investigation sounded harmless enough, and I decided to help this woman with her possible ghost.

I knocked on the door rather loudly to be sure the elderly woman would hear. When she ominously opened the chained door just a crack, with her eyes sullen and fierce, I feared she may be living in a distorted reality.

The white-haired old lady looked up at me strangely and gruffly said, "You looking for somebody?"

"We are looking for Lilly. I am Marcia . . . we spoke on the phone."

"Oh, yes, I remember. Come on in, but close the door and lock it. I have the air conditioner running." We quickly brought our equipment bags inside, as threatening weather was imminent.

The small red brick house had a large picture window in the living room, where sheer curtains hung the entire length behind the open solid-color drapes. Every window in the house had metal blinds installed that Lilly said helped insulate the house.

I turned on my digital recorder and proceeded to explain the permission form Lilly needed to sign before we conducted the investigation. After gaining proper initials and her signature, I stated that I was already recording audio and the recorder was on the table next to her chair. "We do that in case we capture something otherworldly while we set up," I said.

"The ghost is not here now," said Lilly. "He was here this afternoon, but he's not here now."

"Did he know we were coming?"

"No. I think he picked up on my telephone calls. That's how I think he gets my information. Like when I talk to the police, if I get real upset about the ghost, I'll call them and they'll come over and he'll be down there playing," she said. "I think he has a tape recorder, but I can't find his speaker down there. He will turn whatever he is playing off, and then I go down there and he is gone. He made himself invisible, I guess."

"Have you ever seen him with your eyes?"

"I saw a knee and a foot. He was down there in the reclining chair, and evidently he was taking a nap and he heard me open the basement door and he got himself all out of sight except for that knee down to the foot. He had on black slacks and black shoes, and that's all I ever saw of him," she said.

"What happened next?" I asked.

"He got up and walked away. I didn't go down."

"Is there another way out of the basement?"

"No, no other way out but up those stairs."

As Lilly got up and walked to the smallest of the three bedrooms, her progress slow and halting, Lisa and I exchanged a glance, acknowledging we both felt a warning signal about our client's behavior.

The room was used as a TV room, and Lilly had gone to turn off the television. When she called us into the room, we saw it was furnished like a den, with a small couch and two aging recliners. There was a second door that opened to the landing of the stairs that led to the basement. Not only did that doorknob have a key lock, but there was also a locking latch a few inches below the knob. I asked her why she had a lower latch on that door, and she matter-of-factly said, "To keep the ghost from getting in from the basement."

Suddenly and without warning, a streak of lightning split the sky and thunder shook the house, startling us all. "Holy shitballs!" Lisa exclaimed.

As Lisa and I regained our composure, we noticed Lilly was gone. How could a decrepit old woman leave a room unnoticed in only a matter of seconds? I called out, "Lilly? Where are you?"

"I'm in the living room," her low and shaky voice said, as we heard the clanking of the metal as she lowered the blinds. "I'll be right back. I want to show you what the ghost did to my recliner."

As she slowly made her way back into the room, using her cane more like a crutch, I was wondering if what I had dismissed as bizarre was really insanity at work. I took note of everything about her. She was plump, dressed in blue jeans with an elastic waist that was obviously for comfort around the girth of her midriff. Her lightweight red sweater was nearly threadbare where the tips of her breasts, in her white bra, were almost showing through. Her short, white hair hung in a bob-style haircut, and she wore fuzzy pink house slippers on her feet.

With labored breathing Lilly walked to the recliner at the furthest point of the room, laid her cane against the TV stand, and put her hands on top of the recliner, ever so gently pulling it forward so we could see behind. There was a circular board that held the swivel rocker-recliner that seemed to have come loose from the bottom of the chair. Lilly noticed we were not so concerned about it, and suddenly and swiftly the ninety-year-old woman picked up the heavy recliner, putting the bottom of the chair in our full view. She said, "The ghost took off the round bottom of the recliner! Do you see those four holes? That's where the screws go, and the ghost took the screws out!"

Once again startled, but not from the storm raging outside, we said, "Yes, Lilly, we see it."

Lisa said, "I'm so sorry, Lilly." It was at this point that Lisa and I realized we were dealing with someone with an unsound mind—non compos mentis: not sane or in one's right mind.

As we left to return to the living room, Lilly stopped and took off an elastic band bracelet from her wrist that held several keys and locked the front bedroom door. That room is where she stored her extra household supplies on the bed.

"I'm sorry this room is such a mess. I fell down the basement stairs, and they brought everything up and piled it in that room. I can't go down in the basement anymore. I haven't been down there for three years." If she hadn't been down there in three years, how did she go down and search for the speaker to the ghost's tape recorder?

It was then we noticed that all the doorknobs in the house, including the bathroom, had key locks on the outside of each door, enabling her to lock people "in," but she insisted it was to keep the ghost out. By this time I had set up a tripod and video camera and had a digital recorder running in the other room. We couldn't just bolt and leave over $2,000 of equipment behind, even though that was our immediate thought. We persevered, in hope that our imaginations were overreacting. We took a deep breath and decided to continue with the investigation.

Lilly sat in her chair in the living room and began telling us about the ghost that had been there for three years. "The ghost steals stuff, and the police won't do anything about it," she said. "So far I've lost thousands of dollars' worth of items. About fifteen of my good blouses were taken and replaced with cheap ones. My six-foot ladder was taken and replaced with an eighteen-foot ladder. I don't need one that big," said Lilly. "Then my gun came up missing."

"Your gun?" I asked.

"Yes. I had a handgun—a .32-caliber revolver. I kept it in my bedroom, and it came up missing. A week later the ghost put a bigger gun in its place. I didn't want a bigger gun," said Lilly.

"The ghost knocks on the basement door wanting in, and I get frightened," she continued. Upon our arrival we had heard what sounded like knocking, and it continued off and on throughout our visit. We discovered that her folding dropleaf dining room table was situated over an air vent. When the air conditioner was on, the dropleaf swayed just enough to gently bang into the wall, causing a knocking sound; however, we continued to hear the knocking off and on when the air conditioner was not running, and it did sound like it was coming from the basement.

What we didn't know at that time was that Lilly had called the police to come to her house thirteen times within three months. According to the police reports, an officer was dispatched for each of the following: complainant heard someone knocking on her basement door from the inside of her house; someone kept stealing things from elsewhere and putting items in her garage; she had a loaded gun in her bedroom, which would be put away when the police came; someone was trying to pry open her bedroom window; someone stole her gun and put a different one in its place; someone was hammering in her basement, and her other gun had been stolen; nobody was taking her seriously, and noises were still coming from her basement; a male was in her basement playing a tape recorder; and more.

Lilly continued telling us what havoc the ghost in the basement created. "I locked my bedroom door and was lying in my bed. Luckily I hadn't fallen asleep yet when the ghost, a man, walked through the TV room wall into my bedroom. He disturbed my cat, and the cat started running around the room and must have scared him, 'cause the ghost backed out," she said. "Then I could hear six people talking in the TV room. All of them left except for one guy and one girl. He was trying to talk her into having sex in the front bedroom. The girl said she had never done anything like that and he talked her into it, saying it wouldn't hurt. They had sex every day for a long time, and I would get up and wash the bedclothes each day, 'cause I didn't want that sex smell in my house. That is when I began sleeping in my street clothes. Having a strange man in my house, I wasn't going to put on a nightgown."

By this time Lilly seemed exhausted, and Lisa and I felt the need to at least check out the basement. We told Lilly to rest in her chair, but she quickly got up to get another set of keys to unlock the doors in the basement. As we stood in the kitchen, and before handing me the keys, Lilly again told us that she'd had a terrible fall down the basement stairs and had not been in the basement since.

"I was heading down the steps to the laundry room when I fell. I have no memory of it. To this day I do not have any idea who found me. When I woke up, I was in the hospital," said Lilly.

"How do you do your laundry then?" I asked.

"Oh, I hire a woman who comes once a month. She starts my first load of laundry, then goes to the store to get my groceries for the next month. I like those frozen dinners pretty good."

"Does she clean your house too?"

"Oh, no, I do all my own cleaning. I try to control the ghost with the sweeper. He doesn't like it when I run it."

Lilly had mentioned earlier that she had lost her husband fourteen years before. Lisa said, "If I may ask, how did your husband pass away?"

Her head lowered, and she quietly said, "A skull fracture. He fell in the driveway four or five times. Every time he fell, it must have broke it again or something."

This not making much sense, Lisa asked if he'd had a stroke.

"No."

I asked, "Do you think he had several mini-strokes, to make him fall down so many times?"

"The hospital never mentioned anything about any strokes. He just kept falling and hitting the same part of his head each time."

Lisa and I both feared Lilly may have played a role in the demise of her husband, but we had no idea how and we had no proof.

More brave than sensible, Lisa and I took the keys from Lilly and headed downstairs (after unlocking the doorknob and another bolt latch that led to the stairs). Knowing Lilly did her own housecleaning and she hadn't been downstairs for years, we expected the basement to be full of dust and in disarray, but it was very clean and tidy. Lilly stood at the top of the stairs, directing us to the light switch. Lilly asked, "Is it clean down there?"

"Yes, ma'am, it is very clean down here," Lisa answered.

The room Lilly called the "rec room" had a treadmill, a card table with a jigsaw puzzle started, several chairs, a mini kitchen, and a half bath connected to the laundry room. There was a locked door that we were told housed a tool and furnace room. We found no possible source of the knocking sound that we had heard upstairs through the vent. Then we saw something strange and disturbing: two tiny rocking chairs sitting side by side at the far end of the room, both displaying an old-fashioned doll from the 1940s era. They looked like large composite dolls, one with (once) blinking eyes. Both had cloth bodies and were wearing plain, faded dresses. One doll had more cracks and damage to the face than the other, making it appear grotesque and very creepy as a result. Upon seeing this unexpected display, Lisa quietly exclaimed, "What the hell is that?"

Suddenly we both had a weird feeling of danger, and our desire to see what was behind the locked door faded into oblivion. We noticed not only that the tiny basement windows were useless for an escape, if necessary, but that Lilly had also once again disappeared.

In a madhouse sanity looks crazy, and we felt that insanity had stolen her mind like a thief! We feared we were on the verge of being locked in that basement. We truly felt the gun was still in the house. I'm not sure who made it up the stairs first, but in an instant we were both standing in the kitchen, finding Lilly rustling a paper bag closed and stuffing it back into her kitchen drawer.

Lisa talked to Lilly as I quickly packed my equipment. When asked about the dolls in the basement, Lilly said those were her childhood dolls. Then she shared that she had given birth to twin boys who died at birth, but she said there was no relevance to the two dolls in the matching rocking chairs in the basement. Lilly buried her twin boys in a local cemetery, never giving them names. Her husband is buried there, and her plot is awaiting her arrival, where she will be placed between her twins.

The storm had passed, and we started thinking our way out of this mess. Lisa gave Lilly some caring advice, assuring her that her loved ones were near. We quickly said our goodbyes and left. Backing out of the driveway, I turned the wrong direction, and as we went back by the house to leave the plat, we saw Lilly peering out of her blinds from the living room. Abandoning isn't my thing, but this was different. I knew we had to get away.

Once I was safely home, adrenaline flooded my system. Trying to sleep was useless. I uploaded the audio and video from the investigation onto my computer. I filed the consent form Lilly had signed, giving us permission to enter her home and conduct a paranormal investigation. I had verbally told her we were recording audio the minute we entered her house.

With headphones on and in the first few minutes of the recorded audio, there it was: not a ghostly voice, but Lilly's confession. As Lisa and I walked into another room, my recorder was on the table next to Lilly. Sitting in her chair, she quietly said, "I murdered."

Once again, fear found me. I didn't fear the unknown, but I did fear the human factor of mental illness. Did we escape confinement and pure, unadulterated terror?

There was no ghost in Lilly's house. Her ghostly encounter may have been attributed to dissociative identity disorder, likely caused by severe trauma, such as extreme, repetitive physical, sexual, or emotional abuse. Was she the young girl being talked into having sex with a man when she didn't want to? Or did she do some permanent brain damage when she fell down the stairs three years earlier (the exact number of years the ghost had been coming around)? Did she have anything to do with her husband falling and dying of a skull fracture?

Three days later I called Lilly and was going to talk

bluntly about our findings and ask the hard questions. When she answered the phone, she said, "I'm not feeling well today and don't want to answer any questions. Thanks for calling." After much thought, we closed the case.

Lilly called several weeks later and left a message that she now had three ghosts and that we should come back out. We made the mistake of speaking to her conscious mind when it was the mind underneath that needed to talk, but that was the job of a medical professional. I prayed that Lilly would one day escape her prison without walls.

TWO

Unexpected Deprivation

Seven years earlier . . .

The stars were almost nonexistent as clouds blanketed the dark winter sky, trying their best to hide the crescent moon that had little light to shine. The temperature had dropped to a crisp twenty-seven degrees, and frost crystals were forming on the windowpanes in elaborate patterns.

As I was chatting on the phone, I heard the loud squeak of the front door as it opened and closed, bringing a sigh of relief that my son, Danny, was finally home. Relief quickly turned to worry when I heard the bathroom door in the basement close and lock just moments after he arrived.

It was no secret that I suspected drug use. I stealthily approached the bathroom door and quickly knocked. Upon hearing my knock on the door, Danny emerged, asking what I wanted. He stood in the hall, and I searched him. All the while he was laughing, even offering to drop his pants, if necessary. He did an about-face, as if in the military, still wittily mocking my insistence. I also searched the bathroom, to no avail. He lightheartedly inquired if he could continue using the bathroom, and looking at each other, we jubilantly laughed.

Feeling a bit overbearing, yet reassured, I ascended the second flight of stairs of our trilevel home. Suddenly a clairsentient feeling consumed me. I had a clear perception that something was wrong. I felt the energy pulsate up my spine. It was a bone-tingling feeling of simultaneous love and sadness. I had the "all-knowing" feeling that Danny was gone.

Instinctively I grabbed a screwdriver, woke my husband out of a sound sleep, and ran downstairs. I tried to open the door, but it was locked. I called out to Danny as I violently beat on the bathroom door, with no response. My heart pounded as my husband pried the door open with the screwdriver. When the door gave way, we saw Danny's body slumped on the floor, and his head gently fell backward into my husband's hands. The syringe he had used to inject heroin lay on the floor near his feet. "He's down," my husband yelled. "Call 9-1-1!"

While I spoke to the emergency dispatcher, I saw my son's lips turn blue. She said to begin mouth-to-mouth resuscitation, but I was hysterical. My husband performed it. I stood alone in the darkness of the family room as I waited for help to arrive; I realized that my life was at the point of crisis.

My husband stepped away from his lifesaving attempts when help arrived. The EMTs administered two doses of naloxone (Narcan) and performed CPR and mouth-to-mouth for twenty-three minutes before I heard the words, "Call it." Then I felt nothingness.

"I'm sorry, ma'am. We did everything we could," said one of the EMTs. "The coroner is on his way."

At that moment I vaguely perceived his words. Things were occurring too quickly for me to clearly understand. My mind was in total stillness while life was passing by in a blur of motion.

My husband put his arm around me and gently whispered, "I'm so sorry." My first instinct was to jerk myself away. If I didn't succumb to sympathy, the events that had just occurred may not actually have happened. But the unspoken voices urged me to receive his sympathy in kindness, as my desire for another ending was an anticipatory oversight on my part.

The reality was that my youngest child, my only son, was dead.

I lost Danny when he was thirty-two. On December 18, I inadvertently joined many other mothers in what has been dubbed the Grief Club, the club of the brokenhearted. The one association every mother prays to avoid. A child's death changes the natural order of things, and for those who have experienced it, it literally turns their world upside down.

It felt like the life force that sustained me could not bear the fact that my precious child would never draw breath again. I felt my soul would be forever lost in grief.

My world was shattered beyond repair. Initially I felt numb, which may have been my mind's way of shielding me from the pain. The numbness alternated with disbelief and denial. It was around one thirty in the morning when I found myself sitting on the edge of the recliner in the living room as the coroner wheeled out the body bag that carried my son's remains. The sound of the screen door's closing echoed through my head. I felt a bit out of reality, in a state of surrealism. As I somberly drifted into an altered state of consciousness, the events that had led to this tragic night began to play through my mind.

Danny was my second child—a baby I wasn't sure I would ever have, after my first, a daughter named Jennifer, who seemed to be born with the powerful burst of energy of a whirlwind. When she found it impossible to sleep, I would rock her in the dead of night. When Jennifer grew to the toddler stage and finally slept through the night, I decided it was time to give her a sibling.

Born on April 20, 1982, Daniel Andrew's bright blue eyes found mine, although I'm sure I looked a little blurry to him. He laughed, as only a baby can laugh, a sweet sound unblemished by the pain that life can bring.

When I think of Danny as a young child, he was always the first to find and make a new friend; his heart was bigger than the moon. His gentle soul revealed a person whose natural disposition was quiet, refined, and tender. He enjoyed being a kid. An unknown future lay before him, but he didn't care what that future would be. He was just fascinated with the world.

When he was two, I divorced and received custody of both of my children. I remarried a year later. My second husband and I had five children between us, their ages ranging from three to fourteen. Our situation—the blended family—was pretty stereotypical in America.

We moved from Ohio to Florida six months before Danny started kindergarten. When we settled in Vero Beach, it was a quiet beachside town—a bedroom community, meaning that it had few major employment centers. There were no malls or large retail stores—just banks, restaurants, small shops, and grocery stores. To do any major shopping, we had to drive forty-five minutes either north to the city of Melbourne or south to Fort Pierce.

Located along Florida's Atlantic Coast, Vero Beach boasted a few resort-like hotels, golfing, and of course, beaches. The main attraction of Vero Beach at that time was that the Los Angeles Dodgers conducted their spring training (February and March) at the facility known as Dodgertown at Holman Stadium.[1] Now being locals, living just a mile away from the stadium, we took the kids to many of their games, almost always getting an autograph from one of the Dodgers. My children went to Dodgertown Elementary School, which held all the important award ceremonies and elementary school graduations at the stadium.

Danny struggled with school throughout his entire elementary career. He needed constant assistance and tutoring just to maintain average grades. After seven years of living and growing up in Vero Beach, we returned to Ohio, where he started back in school in the sixth grade. He considered himself a Floridian, and with his tanned skin and surfer-cut blond hair, he wasn't fitting in so easily in this known preppy community.

I contacted the principal of the middle school that he was now attending to inquire about special help and testing that may be available. This was long before any type of legislation existed to hold schools accountable; parents really had no input on assessments and intervention. I was matter-of-factly told no by the principal. "If you feel there is a need to have your child tested for any type of disability, you must do so yourself in the private sector," she stated, having no problem telling me that there were no mandates or laws for the school to do so.

I managed to arrange specialized testing with professionals at the Children's Medical Center of Dayton.[2] Results of extensive private sector testing revealed that Danny had auditory processing dysfunction (APD) and attention deficit disorder (ADD).

With the appropriate paperwork in hand, I again met with the principal of the middle school. I provided the official diagnoses and asked what could be done to help my son. Once more I was versed on the lack of current laws and mandates. I reminded her that I had followed through with the testing she recommended. "Mrs. Treadway," she said, "we are not required by law to either test or address these issues."

"My son obviously needs help and at least concessions in the classroom!" I exclaimed.

"I'm sorry, but you will have to assist him at home," she said, in an arrogant tone.

I wasn't aware that there were actually steps I could have taken at that time, but a legal process had to be followed to make them happen. Danny soon began the slow descent to academic failure.

The issues that reared their heads during middle school became more complex for Danny in high school. He was feeling like an outsider, overlooked by almost everyone, making him feel invisible in the classroom. He continued to struggle and was classified as a low achiever who was failing because he was so far behind the others. The implementation of the Improving America's Schools Act—an education reform act to help disadvantaged students and hold schools accountable—didn't come soon enough to be of assistance to my son. Danny did not successfully complete his high school career.

Being a teenager, feeling ineffective and living in such a toxic culture doesn't make life easy. Everyone has a heartbreaking story, and Danny's continued, as he and a few friends began experimenting with drugs and alcohol.

These boys hung at the parks and basketball courts. Sometimes they swore, told jokes (often at the expense of one of their friends—no offense taken), or talked of problems at school, but companionship and camaraderie were in abundance. And on occasion, so were cigarettes and alcohol. When marijuana was introduced to the group, they had to find a more secretive spot to meet.

~

As the boys matured, doing their best to become responsible, they all jumped on life's Ferris wheel and married. Four had children, three later divorced, and one remarried. It appeared that everyone had overcome the drug and alcohol dependence that began as teenagers . . . with the exception of Danny, although he did his best to control his addiction.

Danny and his girlfriend eventually married and had a baby boy. He gained a stepdaughter from that union—a marriage that didn't last very long—but his relationships with his son and stepdaughter were a gift that he cherished the rest of his life.

After his divorce Danny moved back home. We were midlife parents, with Danny, an adult child, living with us. He had an addiction problem that continued into adulthood. It happens in the best of families. Substance abuse issues had gotten so out of hand with Danny that I insisted he seek some type of help. I had to force the issue, and he finally obliged. He successfully completed an inpatient rehabilitation program. Although he occasionally consumed alcoholic beverages and smoked cigarettes, his illegal drug use ceased.

During his recovery Danny worked for a landscape company. His children were over regularly. His life involved mostly watching TV, working, and hanging with his kids.

He enjoyed cooking; his favorites were cabbage rolls, chicken and dumplings, and homemade beef jerky.

Danny was nearing two years heroin free, when suddenly an old friend started coming around again. What I didn't know was that this "friend" was using, and he would soon seduce Danny back into the squalid clutches of heroin. You see, users like company.

When I realized he had a problem again, I constantly talked to him (mostly yelled) about seeking treatment. But as an adult, he had to agree to treatment, which he didn't at that time. Even the local crisis center had a waiting period of two weeks.

I decided it was time to stop the yelling and simply be kind. We were way beyond the tough love concept (which I wasn't tough enough to do anyway). I didn't stop the quest of his getting well; I just didn't yell.

I made the decision to have some fun and make memories. We booked a trip to Disney World: my husband and I, Danny and his two children. I faced some backlash about this decision. "Why are you rewarding bad behavior?" I just knew it was the right thing to do, and it was a wonderful trip.

I finally convinced Danny to enter a rehabilitation program. At last there was some hope for a better future.

A better future was not ours to see. Addiction kept manifesting itself in his life. If it wasn't heroin, it was alcohol. Before I could help him choose a treatment option, he was gone.

He had been drinking that night, the night he died.

He didn't know that combining alcohol and heroin was a very dangerous matter, as both are central nervous system depressants that can cause death. I later found out from the doctor who performed the autopsy that the alcohol level in Danny's blood was way above the legal limit; and when the drug was injected, his breathing instantly stopped. Had he not combined the two substances, he would not have died that night.

Losing my son tore apart my heart, and my emotions bounced back and forth like the steel ball inside a pinball machine. But I was in charge—in charge of everything: deciding on funeral arrangements, the wake, writing my own farewell, and consoling my family. I will never forget watching my son's little boy uncontrollably grieve for his father, while his daughter sat quietly, as anger began her emotional stages of grief. I felt helpless as I watched my daughter, his sister, cry while slumped in a chair at my dining room table, her head hanging slightly above a puddle of tears. I was going to have to help them through the grief process as I worked to help myself learn to face this tragic loss and, hopefully, one day embrace life again.

Danny died the day after his son's twelfth birthday and seven days before Christmas. The soonest we could have held his funeral was Christmas Eve, but I didn't want to forever think of his funeral as part of the holiday each year. We held the funeral eleven days after his death.

Death wasn't kind. It snatched my child, who was far too young to die. As I sat in the recliner on the night he died, I counted the times our souls smiled together. Danny will forever live in my heart. I learned that death isn't the end; it is only the end of a chapter . . . like this one.

Notes

1. Wikipedia, Historic Dodgertown. https://en.wikipedia.org/wiki/Historic_Dodgertown
2. Wikipedia, Dayton Children's Hospital. https://en.wikipedia.org/wiki/Dayton_Children%27s_Hospital

GHOSTLY ENCOUNTERS

THREE

In Pursuit of the Truth

The night Danny died, I lay in my bed enveloped in silence; it was nearing three o'clock in the morning as sleep pooled in my eyes, along with the tears. I fought it with everything I had, as this night sleep was unwelcome. In the silence I could hear the winter wind blowing outside, stirring my emotions and warning of the darkness that was to come. I had no control over it because it wasn't mine to control.

In the stillness my soul painfully grieved the loss of my son. I lay there in the night as thoughts flowed through my mind. My paranormal and spiritual journey was not such an enigma anymore. The journey wasn't easy; it was lonely—even painful at times—and comfort wasn't guaranteed. Throughout my search I found the truth. What I was now looking for was peace. I tucked the blanket tight under my chin, as my thoughts drifted to how my journey in pursuit of the truth began in hope of keeping sleep at bay.

I had been working in the small town of Bellbrook since 1998, first as a newspaper reporter and later as a school district employee. These jobs enabled me to get to know the community and local government officials.

Bellbrook is a small, rural town about eleven miles from where I live. As a school district employee, I watched my grandkids participate in various school district events. One year my eight-year-old granddaughter and her friend dressed up as clowns and rode on a float in the Sugar Maple Parade, passing out candy and school information. I truly enjoyed serving as the school-community relations coordinator for Bellbrook-Sugarcreek Schools.[1]

Shortly before my job ended, I began researching the history of Bellbrook and exploring unexplained activity in this spirited little town. I developed an insatiable desire to know what or who was making its presence known and why. At first I felt I was the one seeking proof of the unknown out of curiosity, but now I wonder if I was put on this path for a reason: to help me understand that there is an afterlife, to better prepare me for the ultimate sorrow—the death of my own child.

There was a fair amount of criticism and controversy about the belief in ghosts when I began participating in paranormal investigating. The paranormal reality television series *Ghost Hunters* was starting its fifth year and gaining popularity. Admittedly the little bit that I watched truly scared me, yet I was strangely hooked—not on the show, but on the existence of the supernatural realm itself. I realized it wasn't curiosity; it was the intense feeling that I knew—or used to know—something. It was just on the tip of my tongue, so to speak. I think I felt this way because I'd once had what I believe to have been a near-death experience, when my blood level dropped to a dangerously low level and I was rushed to the hospital for a blood transfusion. After my survival I wasn't sure what I had experienced—the near end to my human life or the beginning of the next?

Everything began with a "just for fun" ghost hunt in a former school building for two graduating students who experienced several puzzling occurrences while doing scholarship community service work for the Bellbrook-Sugarcreek Family Resource Center (FRC).[2] The FRC was located in the former Sugarcreek Elementary building. It had been constructed as a high school and opened in 1925; an addition was built in 1939.[3] The building last served as an elementary school in 2007. The district had rented the space to churches and community service organizations ever since.

The students, JR and Andy, both had their own unexplainable paranormal experiences while volunteering at the FRC, although JR, Andy, and Susan, the center's director at the time, all experienced an occurrence together. They were standing at the counter in the room that had served as the office of the former school. The boys were standing in the secretary's area, on the side where wooden cabinet doors for under-counter storage were. Susan was standing on the opposite side of the counter. They were engaged in conversation when suddenly one of the cabinet doors popped open. At that exact time, one of Susan's pierced earrings fell out of her ear. It didn't just drop; it landed behind her. It would have taken some force for the earring and the back to end up where they did. The three of them were befuddled, and the boys immediately initiated efforts to try to duplicate the cabinet door's opening, to no avail.

Susan procured permission to hold the students' graduation gift of a ghost hunt and recruited two more adults to chaperone: her good friends Chris, then the director of the Bellbrook-Sugarcreek Chamber of Commerce, and myself. The investigation was set for June 19, 2008, my younger brother's birthday (who had died two years earlier).

I had been suffering for several years from periodic bouts of anemia, which could make me feel extremely tired and weak. The day of the investigation, I was feeling pretty feeble. I had planned on bringing all of the camera equipment that I used on the job, but I'd felt too weak to carry it all myself. I enlisted the help of my adult son, Danny. Although he wasn't thrilled when I asked him to attend the ghost hunt, he went with me out of the goodness of his heart.

I stood there gazing at the three-story building as my son unloaded the camera bags and equipment. I'd been in this building hundreds of times, but this evening something felt different. It wasn't my job bringing me here tonight.

The red brick structure had remained essentially the same over the years. The front entrance used to be the center focal point of the building, until the addition shifted it to the left. The notably large windows were cosmetically boarded up, leaving a diminutive opening and vastly limiting the view.

We arrived in the early evening. As we entered the front door, I could hear a rumble of thunder off in the distance, although it never rained and no bad weather was forecasted. The graduates were very excited and anxious to put to the test some tricks that they had learned watching the paranormal TV shows.

It was still daylight as I set up the camcorder on a tripod in front of the same cabinet that had previously opened on its own—an old wooden door that hung slightly crooked on its hinges. The loose hinges actually made the door shut more tightly, because it had to be pushed into the closed position. JR and Andy demonstrated that the door would not open even when they jumped up and down on the floor or when dropping something heavy on top of the counter. We left the room, with the camcorder running.

As darkness fell, we spent a little over three hours pretty much scaring each other. I remember walking into a dark room and screaming when I found myself face to face with what I thought was someone lurking in the shadows. In actuality it was a 5-foot-tall dark brown stuffed animal: the mascot of the FRC! Everyone laughed as I stood there, waiting for my heart rate to return to normal.

We decided to stay together as a group and went to the lower level armed with nothing but a digital camera. We went room to room, snapping pictures. Upon quick review of the photographs, nothing seemed to be show-ing up . . . until near the end of the series. We were all startled to see a tiny white ball of light in the lower right corner of one photo. Our astonishment continued when it did not show up in the next photo, taken immediately after. "Wow!" Andy exclaimed. "We got something!" It was nearing one o'clock in the morning. The group decided to take a break and ascended the stairs to the third floor, to the room known as the "couch room."

As we enjoyed refreshments, Danny picked up my dig-ital camera, and he and JR went outside to walk around the building. They exited the door on the south side, propping it open with a block of wood to be sure they would not be locked out. The outside door was situated on a landing between the lower and second levels of the building. A large, carpeted floor mat with a rubber backing was placed inside, behind the door entrance.

About fifteen minutes later, Danny and JR burst into the room and breathlessly began telling us that they had just experienced something they could not explain! They were behind the building, standing in the empty asphalt parking lot, when they both thought they saw a shadow of a person inside one of the windows on the lower level, behind the stage area in the gym. A fourteen-foot-high fence surrounded the area behind them, where the school district used to park school buses. Inside the locked fence enclosure, a trailer was parked, and a truck topper was lying on the ground. Danny was in the process of taking a photo of the window when he and JR heard a sound behind them.

It was loud, like metal hitting metal. Danny just happened to be holding the camera shutter button down halfway (in focus mode), as he turned around to see what made the sound. The boys did not see anything with their own eyes, but then Danny noticed that something was showing up in the viewfinder of the digital camera. While they saw nothing directly, the viewfinder displayed a blue and green light hovering near the ground, next to the truck topper. Danny immediately pushed the shutter button and captured the now rising three-part light, about four feet in the air. Still not seeing anything, Danny once again partially pressed the shutter button and found the light about 2 feet above the fourteen-foot fence; he quickly snapped another photograph. By the time the camera was ready for another shot, the light could not be found.

Just as speedily as the boys had run upstairs with this news, everyone ran downstairs but found no evidence of the extraneous illumination. The boys immediately began discussing possible extraterrestrials, while the chaperones were thinking about the probability that it may have been something from Wright-Patterson Air Force Base,[4] located only seventeen miles from Bellbrook. Whatever it was, the boys had proof: two photos on the camera. We huddled together, as the time drew near two o'clock in the morning, to review the photos.

In the first photo, the brilliance of the light was indeed visible against the dark of the night. We could easily see that there were three parts to the light. The colors from left to right were dark blue, light blue, and green. The three lights appeared a bit elongated, but it was possible that the camera may have been moving slightly when Danny took the photograph. The truck topper and top fence rail were visible, proving that the boys' account was accurate.

The second, sharper photo showed the same brilliance and colors. The shape of the lighted anomaly—now approximately sixteen feet above the ground—resembled a large dumbbell.

As we entered the building through the door that we had left propped open, Chris noticed water droplets all over the steps heading to the lower level. It was odd, because it had never rained and the carpeted mat on the landing was completely dry. Upon closer examination, the first and last steps were not wet. Two footprints could be seen in the water. It appeared that someone had just walked in from the rain, but that was impossible because it did not rain. We closed the door and checked all unlocked rooms in the school, finding nobody there. Pipes running alongside the wall were dry. We could not find a water source for the mysterious occurrence. None of us were carrying water bottles. What water we had was upstairs in the room on the third floor.

As we packed the equipment by the cabinet door (which never opened), we kept trying to figure out what the unexplainable phenomena could have been, but we could not explain the unexplainable. We were just as perplexed about these experiences as we were excited. This evening was going to end with more questions than answers, but it was an evening that none of us would ever forget.

Now possessing an even greater desire to find out more about unexplained natural or supernatural phenomena such as we had experienced, I set out in search of any secrets that may be lurking behind the doors of the Sugarcreek Elementary building.

A few weeks later, on a day just like every other day, I found myself at the Family Resource Center. Susan informed me about John's upcoming retirement. John was the building custodian. It had been my intention to one day talk to him and inquire about whether he'd ever had any unusual encounters while working alone in the building. Apparently time was now of the essence.

I returned to the building when John's shift was well underway, finding him in the gymnasium, pushing a large dust mop. He was near the center of the gym when I got his attention. Knowing John only as an acquaintance, I suddenly found myself stammering for words. It isn't every day that you ask someone you hardly know if there are spirits of the dead looming around.

"Hello," I said. "I hear you are getting ready to retire."

"Yes, and I'm looking forward to it," he replied.

"What are your plans?"

"I'm going to catch up on my hobby, woodworking."

"That's interesting. I wish you the best of luck. I'm actually here to ask you something."

"What's that?"

"I hope you will be honest with me, and I'll explain after I ask you."

"Okay," he said hesitantly.

"Have you ever seen or heard things happening in this building that you can't explain?"

"You mean like ghosts?"

"I mean like experiencing something that you can't provide an explanation for."

John propped both his hands on top of the mop handle and sighed. "You know, I'm Catholic, and Catholics are not supposed to believe in this stuff."

"So, is that a yes?"

"Well . . . let me tell you that several teachers have told me they've seen a little boy wearing old clothing, like knickers, as they were walking to the office. Not on the same day or anything—several teachers, all at different times."

"Have you ever seen him?"

"No."

"You are alone in the building a lot. Have you experienced anything?"

"I shouldn't talk about this, but since you asked, I will."

John pointed to what used to be the stage. Now enclosed, it had once been used as a classroom, when the district needed more learning space. At this time it was being used for storage. There was a ledge from the enclosed wall to the edge of the stage, where the physical education teacher often lined up six or seven basketballs.

"I don't turn on the vapor lights, because it takes so long for them to get bright. I turn on the side lights, and it is rather dim when I'm working in the gym," he explained. "As I'm dust mopping the gym floor, on many occasions I've heard boxes being stacked in the area that was the stage. I used to stop what I was doing and enter the room, only to find it empty. I don't bother checking anymore."

He continued. "One thing that happened made the hair on the back of my neck stand up." John had my undivided attention. "One day, as I was sweeping, one of the basket-balls fell off the edge of the stage and started rolling in cir-cles. The ball continued to roll, and the circles got smaller and smaller, until the ball was about to stop in the middle of the floor. I didn't think much of it, until I walked over to pick it up. As I started to reach for it, the ball rolled away!"

For a moment no words came from my mouth. I was mesmerized by his personal account of these occurrences. Cold chills washed over me. John had just bared his soul and given me a heads up that there was some kind of strange force in existence within this school building. I realized this must be what they call an intelligent haunting, where spirits knowingly interact with people.

A few days later, Susan and I were standing alone in the gym. I was repeating the information about John's expe-riences when I saw a shadow of a dove flying the entire length of the gymnasium wall. The shadow was quite large, and even though it was daytime, there was little daylight because there were no windows in the gym. The only access to sunlight outside was through a small exhaust fan in the opposite wall; however, it only spread enough light on a small portion of the wall and would not explain a shadow going from one end of the gym to the other.

Upon seeing this I had stopped talking, and before I said anything else, Susan said, "I saw it too."

About six months later, I was made aware that the gymnasium in the Sugarcreek Elementary building would soon be rented to a newly formed church. A few friends of mine joined me for one last investigation before the gym would no longer be available.

In the center of the gym floor, I set a Mini Maglite flashlight, turned just enough to remain off. (We do this to make it easier for spirits to make the connection internally to manipulate the flashlight.) I turned on my camcorder, set it in infrared mode, hit record, and set it on the floor facing the flashlight, about twenty feet away. I began a conversation.

"We figured there had to be some people hanging around here," I said.

The flashlight turned on and stayed on.

"Thank you. I'm wondering if you're happy here," I asked. "If you're not happy, turn off the flashlight when I count to three: one, two, three."

The flashlight remained on.

"If you are happy, turn off the flashlight when I count to three."

"One, two" (flashlight started to dim), "three" (flashlight turned off). "Thank you!" I said.

I turned to my friends and said, "You cannot get any more validation than that." That was one of my favorite flashlight communication sessions.

Some say the flashlight action is caused by expansion

and contraction of the reflector—that when you turn on a flashlight, it generates heat and the reflector expands, and after unscrewing the top, it contracts, which causes metal within the flashlight to eventually make contact, turning it on again. In this case the flashlights were kept in the equipment bag, only used for communication. The flashlight was never on long enough to generate any heat. The communication session lasted a total of thirty-one seconds, and for the flashlight to turn off on command was remarkable.

Looking back to when Sugarcreek Elementary was still an active school, I recalled an odd experience that I had inadvertently disregarded. On many occasions my job found me at the office after dark, locking the building after meetings or events. The school district offices were located in a single-story building next to the elementary school. One hallway in the district offices was used as overflow third-grade classrooms for Sugarcreek Elementary. A covered walkway connected the two structures. One night, as I was leaving the one-story building after a meeting, I saw out of the corner of my eye the shadow of a person standing outside the glass doors that led to the elementary. My first thought was that someone had left something behind and was trying to get back into the building. Instinctively I proceeded to open the door, but no one was there. I stepped outside to find the parking lot empty.

Sometime later I was talking to one of the teachers whose classroom used to be in the same hallway as the district offices. I shared my memory, and she quickly grabbed my arm and whispered, "I saw it too!" In that moment relief unleashed within her. "I was in my classroom after dark and needed assistance moving a table. I saw a man walk down the hallway. When I ran after him to ask for help, nobody was there!"

⤴

People usually think of ghosts as frightening and menacing, but that night, when I saw the shadow apparition, it was neither. An instant before there was no one, then there stood the shadow at the back door. In a few seconds, there was no trace of it . . . or anyone.

It was as if it dissolved into the very air itself and blew away with the breeze. Seeing something so surprising and unexpected was hard for my brain to comprehend. I wasn't afraid; it felt more like a knock on a door, inviting me to come have a look.

Notes

1. Bellbrook-Sugarcreek Schools, Bellbrook, OH. https://www.sugarcreek.k12.oh.us
2. Bellbrook-Sugarcreek Family Resource Center (FRC), rebranded to the Bellbrook-Sugarcreek Community Support Center. https://www.bscsc.org
3. Bellbrook Historical Society, *Bellbrook 1816–1981*.
4. Wright-Patterson Air Force Base is located northeast of Dayton, Ohio, and encompasses parts of Greene and Montgomery counties. https://www.wpafb.af.mil

FOUR

Learning the Ropes

The concept of multitasking is doing multiple things simultaneously. Even when multitasking, sometimes there's never enough time in a day.

My daughter, Jennifer, was having that kind of day. After leaving work the last stop was the grocery store in Lebanon, Ohio, before heading home to feed the family. She parked next to a van adorned with a magnetic sign that read "Got Ghosts?" Intrigued, she quickly snapped a photo of the sign with her cell phone.

Jennifer hurriedly loaded her groceries and left, the van still parked beside her. Halfway home she noticed that she didn't have her purse. A bit panicked, she called the number listed on the van, in hope that the occupants were still there and could locate the purse (which she may have left in the cart, next to their vehicle).

"Hello, this is Dave Jones," said the man on the other end of the phone.

"Hi, this is Jennifer. This may sound crazy, but are you still at the grocery store in Lebanon?"

"Uh, yes, I am. Why?"

"I was just there, and I think I may have left my purse in a cart next to your van."

"I see the cart, but there isn't a purse."

"Well, okay then. Thanks."

"No problem."

"You may be wondering how I got your number. I saw your sign about ghosts, and I took a picture to send to my mom. She attended a ghost hunt in Bellbrook and captured some photos that she can't explain. I thought you might take a look at them."

"Sure thing. Have her give me a call."

When she arrived home and was unloading the groceries from her car, Jennifer was relieved to discover that she had left her purse in the trunk.

A few days later, I was still thinking how to explain to a total stranger what we had experienced, when we didn't know ourselves. Finally I phoned Dave, the ghost guy. It was easier than I expected. Although he was a stranger, he was also a ghost hunter; so these things did not seem bizarre to him. I described our experiences and shared the information that John, the school custodian, had given me. Dave was intrigued and requested a date that he and a team member could come to investigate.

We set a date and met. Dave was cofounder of a local paranormal investigation team. Although no other team members attended the investigation, his girlfriend, Jamie

Wilson, was there. It was just the three of us . . . and whatever else dwelled within the walls of the school.

Not knowing exactly what to expect, I was a little fearful, which Dave explained spirits can sense. He carried a digital recording device, in hope of capturing what he called an EVP, which stands for "electronic voice phenomenon." He said that such recordings may be the voices of spirits trying to communicate with us. I was more of a skeptic than a believer. How could that happen? And why couldn't we hear it with our own ears?

We ventured into the gym and down to the boys' locker room. As we descended the stairs, I felt a pressure change; my breathing became heavier, and I had an eerie feeling of gloom. While Dave had a flashlight, he did not want the locker room lights on. Once we were all standing in a secure space, he turned the flashlight off. It was explained to me that in darkness we are able to focus on our other senses. Dave continued to ask questions to anyone who may have been in the spirit world, hoping for responses to be left on the recorder. He called this an EVP session. As he was conducting it, my eyes better adjusted to the darkness. There was just a glimmer of light from the gym; for security reasons several lights throughout the building were permanently left on. Then Dave said that there was something in the bathroom area. I looked and saw a shadow by the sink. It was a short figure, the size of a child. It was just a dark shadow, in the shape of a person. We were standing utterly still, while the shadow moved slightly back and forth as if trying to find someplace to hide.

Just after midnight we were on the second floor in the former office area when I noticed through the window that solar lights in the yard of a house two doors down were randomly flashing on and off. There were about a dozen lights scattered in the front and side of the house, turning on and off with no exact pattern. While Dave and Jamie didn't think much of it, I found this rather odd. I knew solar lights may flicker if not charged properly, but these were not flickering. All of them were turning on and off, one light at a time.

We headed outside, so I could show them where the boys had seen the mysterious lights. Looking at the photographs, Dave felt that what we had captured was more alien than paranormal. That was a can of worms I wasn't ready to open. Calling it a night, he explained to me that it would take some time to review the recorder. He had about three hours of audio, and it would take twice that amount of time to listen and make clips of any possible evidence. He said that he would get back to me in about a week.

A week later Dave called, and he was pleased with his findings. Indeed, he said that he had captured several EVPs and believed there was more than one spirit inhabiting the school building. He wanted to return to the school—this time with video cameras and other devices. I arranged for another ghost hunt. Word had gotten to Chris, Susan, JR, my daughter, and my son-in-law, who all wanted to attend while the ghost hunters were there. Dave brought Patrick DeHart and John Brown, his team members.

Dave played some of the EVPs that he had initially

recorded. One said in a gravelly voice, "Get out," and another one said, "Help me." These words were recorded over a week prior, so telling us to "get out" may not have been as meaningful now; however, hearing that certainly didn't make me feel comfortable. Despite that, there I was, along with eight other people.

The ghost hunters explained that "get out" could mean several things. Sometimes it was a direct response to a question; at other times the spirit was annoyed with human presence. Maybe "get out" was a warning for us to get out, thinking of our safety. Ghost hunters don't take "get out" literally. In fact, it usually leads to additional investigating.

The majority of the people attending were fascinated with the investigation process. I was there because I knew I was supposed to be. I was paying close attention to how these people conducted the investigation, as I felt it was a learning experience for me. What I would later learn is that having too many people at an investigation can cause contamination of evidence. It can be a waste of the investigators' time. That may have been the case for this investigation, until something happened that got everyone's attention!

John and Patrick were on the second floor, walking toward the stairs that went down to the south door. Everyone else was on the lower level, walking toward the stairs that rose to the same door. Conversations were flowing when suddenly a tall, dark figure appeared through the east wall, moved across the landing, and disappeared into the west wall! Everyone screamed, some in fear, some in amazement. Patrick saw a flesh-colored arm that didn't appear to have a hand. It happened so quickly, and as we were just setting up to investigate, no evidence was captured. Dave immediately called Lee Allen, the other cofounder: "Please tell me that you're almost here and you have the static cameras!" After they set up the equipment, the rest of the night was uneventful.

I later checked with a long-time school district employee who knew of a former custodian from her time as a student at the school. She informed me that many years ago, while he was helping clean up from a Fourth of July community celebration, a firework had exploded as he picked it up off the ground, permanently disfiguring his right hand.

⸺

While helping prepare for one of the school's education foundation fundraising events, I was talking to Steve Berryhill, a trustee of the organization. When he asked me what I'd been up to lately, I mustered the courage to tell him about the ghostly experiences. I was prepared to be laughed at. Instead, he quite seriously said, "Oh, I believe."

"Really?" I said.

"Yes. When my kids were young, my son would see apparitions of Native Americans in our basement."

Steve, a well-known member of the community, was also involved with the historical society. He offered to arrange getting us into some historical buildings to investigate.

At the time, Steve lived within walking distance of the

Little Miami River. The Shawnee, Miami, and Wyandot Native American tribes inhabited that area in the early days. Not far from where Steve lived was the birthplace of the famed Shawnee warrior Tecumseh.[1] I found Steve's testimony of his son seeing Native American apparitions entirely plausible.

Steve, the former president of the Bellbrook-Sugarcreek Historical Society,[2] updated a mutual friend of ours, Deborah, about my paranormal activities. Deborah and I had been friends for quite some time. She contacted me to talk about the house that she and her husband owned. They believed their building, located in the heart of Bellbrook, to be haunted.

A log cabin church once stood on the lot where the house is now located. It was torn down to build the house in 1832.[3] A church was built next door, and for many years the house was used as its parsonage. After the church was eventually demolished, the parsonage became a private residence. A man by the name of Eugene Belden lived a long life in that house. He was a member of the Bellbrook City Council from 1932 to 1940. He lived to be an old man; however, he did not die in the house but in a nursing home. Eugene left the house to his caregiver, a woman named Daisy Lansinger, who lived there until her death. Daisy and her daughter-in-law, Betty, were crossing the street to walk to the Bellbrook post office on Christmas Eve, 1976, when they were struck by a vehicle and killed. Daisy was eighty-seven years old, Betty seventy-one.

Deborah and her husband purchased the house to use

as an office. She explained that due to paranormal happenings, they no longer used it as an office but more for storage. Deborah invited me to meet her at the house to show me around.

It was a lovely day when I met Deborah at the house, a two-story structure with clapboard siding. I stepped onto the covered porch, where one stone pillar held the only corner of the roof not supported by the building. Two doors opened onto the porch. The main entrance took you into the living room, and the other to the room that used to be the kitchen.

Deborah showed me around the house. Leaning against a wall were some wood panels and miscellaneous items that she said would mysteriously be moved to a different location the next time she entered. She said the sample planks of wood may be leaning on the south wall of the living room when she left, and the next time she entered, they would be leaning on the west wall of the adjoining room.

The room that she used as an office was upstairs, at the front of the house. She always worked alone. One day she was expecting her husband to arrive to take her to lunch. She heard the creak of the stairs as someone walked up. Thinking that it was her husband, she grabbed her purse and walked out of the room into the open area at the top of the stairs—to find that no one was there.

A small tool shed was attached to the back porch. There was an opening covered by a wood panel secured by a hook and eye. She would frequently find it wide open.

Deborah left the radio on, even when she wasn't there.

Every time she came to work at the office, she would find the radio between stations, with only white noise playing. She would hear messages that were just static on the answering machine.

We went upstairs. The stairs led to the middle of the second floor, a pretty large open area, with one large room at the front of the house and two rooms at the back. The rooms at the back of the house connected to each other; one was quite a bit smaller. Deborah believed that it must have been a nursery, and she decorated the room as such. It was adorned with a Shaker peg rail high on two walls. From one of the pegs hung a primitive doll. On the ledge of the peg rails, she spaced about a dozen spider shells as a decoration. The couple had decided not to use the building as an office anymore when one morning they went upstairs and found all of the shells stacked neatly, one on top of the other, in the middle of the floor.

As we stood in the open area on the second floor, I was so intrigued with what she was telling me that I didn't notice the strange look on her face or perceive what was happening right at that moment. Finally I stopped talking and listened. I looked at Deborah, and before I could say anything, she said, "Yes, Marcia, the walls are knocking. I think someone is trying to get your attention." As soon as I grasped the actuality of what was occurring, the knocking stopped. I was blown away. I realized that I needed to pay closer attention or I may miss exactly what I was looking for. There was only silence after that.

At this point I wasn't even sure what I was looking for. I

realized I needed to be more mindful of what was happening around me. Deborah granted me permission to investigate the house. While waiting for the other investigators, I spent some time sitting in silence and just listening. I quickly learned that I was never truly alone.

I've discovered that a lot of people have an interest in the paranormal but won't talk about it until I bring up the subject. My confidence to broach the subject with people was on the rise.

My friend Jennifer was the head of food service for the school district. I also approached her about what we had experienced. Again to my surprise, she was extremely aware of and interested in the paranormal. In fact, she shared some stories of unexplained happenings in the new middle school that the district had recently built.

Bellbrook Middle School[4] opened its doors for the first time in 2006. Working in a brand new kitchen was great. Jennifer had everything running smoothly before the first student walked through the lunch line. It wasn't long until some of Jennifer's employees and a custodial staff member began reporting odd happenings and Jennifer herself was having experiences.

Before the end of the school day, the cafeteria serving area was secured by industrial pull-down doors. One late afternoon Jennifer and a staff member were working in the office connected to the kitchen, when they both heard a loud sound as if something had fallen. Upon investigation they discovered a heavy sign that had been sitting on a shelf in the serving area lying on the floor. They found it odd that the sign was laying five feet away from the shelf. Had it simply fallen, they thought it should have been right below the shelf.

Custodians would occasionally report to Jennifer that the water faucet to the kitchen sink would be turned on and running when they arrived around five o'clock in the morning. Not every time, but sometimes as they were walking away after turning off the faucet, the water began running again.

What bothered Jennifer the most was walking in the area behind the stage in the "cafetorium." She would get chills up her spine every time and then would feel the need to flee.

The night custodian shared with Jennifer that she felt "something" was in the building, and she named it Windy. She explained that as she swept the floors, she often felt a gust of wind pass by, stirring the pile of dirt that she had just swept. Also, some of the motion sensor toilets would flush for no reason. Jennifer herself had heard this when alone in the building.

As I continued to learn investigation techniques with the ghost hunters, I emailed Jennifer a video that I took of an electronic meter appearing to malfunction during an investigation of a historical house in the township. It was, in fact, playing an off-key electronic version of the hymn "Amazing Grace." Jennifer was alone in her office; and as she opened the video file to view it, the commercial oven in the kitchen began making electronic sounds playing the same song! She could not turn the oven off and had to shut it down from the breaker box. It continued to play the tune of "Amazing Grace" until she did so.

Jennifer and her staff learned to put up with the ghostly antics. She shared these stories with a man from the maintenance department when he was called out to check the faucet and the oven. He was intrigued and, being a longtime resident of the community, researched the history of the property on which the school had been built. It was formerly known as the Tate farm. According to the employee, the elderly man of the family, known as Old Man Tate, had an accident in the small barn. His tractor fell on him, trapping him and causing a slow death. Jennifer acknowledged Old Man Tate and expressed that she felt terrible about the way he had died. After that day the paranormal activity ceased.

It didn't take long for word to spread throughout town that Marcia Treadway was ghost hunting in Bellbrook. I was met with some ridicule, most likely due to the lack of understanding about such phenomena. I soon received a phone call from Barry Tiffany, Sugarcreek Township's administrator,[5] inquiring about what investigations I had coming up and expressing an interest in attending. He said he could also pave the way for future investigations.

I seemed to be creating quite a network of believers, all having their own experiences to report.

Notes

1. Remarkable Ohio, Tecumseh birthplace near intersection of Old Springfield Pike and U.S. 68 in Xenia, Ohio 45385. https://remarkableohio.org/index.php?/category/488

2. Bellbrook-Sugarcreek Historical Society, Facebook. https://www.facebook.com/Bellbrook-Sugarcreek-Historical-Society-186200064787298/

3. Church and parsonage, history and deed information provided by current owners.

4. Bellbrook Middle School, district website https://www.sugarcreek.k12.oh.us.

5. Barry P. Tiffany, Sugarcreek Township Administrator. http://sugarcreekoh.us/index.aspx?nid=92

FIVE

The Reawakening

While my new paranormal experiences had opened the doors to spiritual awakening, they also opened a Pandora's box, in a manner of speaking. It wasn't a box holding evil or illness; it was forgotten, or suppressed, memories. Visions and mystic activity so tangible that I could not believe they were real, so I tucked them away in the back of my mind. I feared what I didn't understand; and I felt that someone, or something, was helping me remember and come to terms with the now ever-flowing recollections.

At the age of twenty-one, I moved into my very own home in north Dayton. It was an older, small, three-bedroom house in a neighborhood of tract housing. It wasn't anything special, but it was mine. Not having been out of my mother's house for very long, I was apprehensive about stepping out of my comfort zone, leaving the sense of safety of the house that I had grown up in.

I spent the first few months getting to know the noises of the house. One consistent noise—hissing in conjunction with a popping sound—concerned me, as a water heater should not make noises like it might explode.

One night I awoke to these sounds and decided to investigate. Before getting out of bed, I looked toward my open bedroom door and saw a dark figure standing in the doorway. This terrified me, but I continued to stare, trying to be sure that I was truly seeing something. The dark shadow figure was tall; it appeared to be a man. His back was leaning on the left side of the doorjamb, with one leg bent and foot propped up, as if relaxed. He was smoking a cigarette. While all I saw was a black shadow, I could discern the red, smoldering end of the lit cigarette. It flickered as he took a slow, long draw. He then tapped the cigarette, as if to dispose of the ashes. Instantly forgetting about the strange sounds of the water heater, I slowly moved the covers up and over my head, as if to hide. When the sun came up, I leaped out of bed to look for ashes or a cigarette butt on the floor . . . but nothing was there. From that moment on, I slept with my bedroom door closed.

As the youngest homeowner on the street, I didn't have anything in common with my immediate neighbors. We didn't communicate, other than an occasional wave.

When I returned home from work one day, I saw an ambulance parked in my neighbor's driveway. He was a man in his 70s. It did not appear, by the lack of activity, to be an urgent need. As I stood on my driveway, however, I witnessed a stretcher being rolled out of the house, covered with a velvet blanket. My neighbor had died, and his body was being removed from the house.

Just then a younger man walked across the yard, directly approaching me. "Hello. I'm the nephew of Jake." I felt terrible that I hadn't even known my neighbor's name.

"Hello," I said. "I am so sorry for your loss. Do you know what happened?"

"My uncle died of lung cancer. He was a lifelong smoker . . . you know, like the guy that used to live in your house."

What? I had no idea who had owned this house before I bought it.

"I don't remember his name, but my uncle told me that he died from emphysema. They were friends and would sit on my uncle's back porch, drinking beer and smoking cigarettes. He died in his home, like my uncle did." He seemed rather matter of fact about what had just happened and explained that he needed to go take care of matters. He asked if I would feed the dog and watch the house. Of course, I obliged.

"Please give me a call if you see anything unusual," he said, as he handed me a piece of paper with his name and phone number.

I felt guilty for not taking the time to get to know my neighbor better, but I did find out more about the former owner of my house. He may have been the shadow whom I saw standing in my doorway. After that I no longer slept with the sheets over my head and my bedroom door closed. I never saw the shadow man again. This happened forty-three years ago, and I had obviously tucked that experience away for a very long time.

I recalled other experiences that became obvious only in hindsight. I was born in the 1950s. My formative years took place during the decade of the hippie, a counterculture of the 1960s. My late teen years ended during the 1970s "Me Decade," a time when things began to feel more peaceful and people wholeheartedly embraced expressing themselves. Some took this as far as what was called "streaking," while others simply owned "pet rocks"—smooth stones from a beach in Mexico that were marketed like live pets.

Parents in the '60s were more involved with their friends and social lives than in spending time with their children. When I was young, there were four neighbors on our street who rotated hosting the "every Friday night" party. Once a month I spent Friday evenings in my bedroom while the adults played their music so loudly that my bedroom wall shook. They would dance, drink, smoke, and tell dirty jokes. All this I could hear, as my bedroom shared the living room wall.

I was eleven years old when I was assigned the task of cleaning up after the hangover-inducing parties. As my parents slept in on Saturday mornings, it was my job to empty the ashtrays and booze glasses. My mother, a chain smoker, saturated our house with the pungent scent of cigarette smoke. In the late '60s, her cigarettes of choice were Virginia Slims.[1] These cigarettes were narrower in circumference and longer than the standard cigarette, to give a more elegant appearance. They were marketed to women, with no regard to the fact that they were the cause of real and serious diseases.

When my parents divorced, my mother's dependence on cigarettes increased. I was now eighteen and still living in my mother's house. I talked to her about the dangers of smoking. She sat at the dining room table, put her cigarette to her lips, and gently sucked the smoke, with a long, steady intake, into her lungs. After holding it there for a moment, she then exhaled. My mother knew proper smoking etiquette, holding the cigarette between her index and middle finger on the filter when she said, "Marcia, I've had a hard life; this cigarette gives me a little bit of pleasure. Please don't deny me the gratification that I get from smoking."

I knew smokers enjoyed their habit because it stimulated the flow of chemicals that made them feel good. I still questioned how anyone could make a habit out of something so fundamentally unpleasant, yet I accepted her choice. It was hers to make.

Ten years later my mother received the diagnosis of lung cancer, and three months later she was dead at the age of fifty-four. I was married, with two young children, ages three and five. Before she died I quit my full-time job and took her on one last vacation to Florida. I became her full-time nurse, and we earnestly discussed every detail of her wishes upon her death. A week before her death, she told me that she had been having dreams about practicing how to fly. "Well, more like floating high around the room," she said. "But I keep bumping into the corners of the walls." We laughed. One of the last things she said to me before her death was "I'm going to miss you."

On July 21, 1987, at 4:45 p.m., I sat by her side, holding her hand as she took her last breath. Upon releasing her hand, I looked up and said, "Watch out for those corners!"

I honored my mother's wishes, arranging for private graveside services. She would be buried in the plot next to her mother. The pastor of the local church officiated the short service. Lost in grief and consoling my young children, I didn't grasp every word, until he began talking about butterflies. The idea expressed by the butterfly is that it has been transformed to eternal life. For people who believe in reincarnation—which my mother did—the butterfly also represents the promise of rebirth. I found the sermon comforting, but what I found extraordinary was watching a pair of butterflies fluttering around her casket during the service, never leaving until we said, "Amen."

My grief was so overpowering that it consumed me. I could not comprehend the loss of my mother at such a young age. She was the only person who loved me unconditionally. I was learning the hard way that dealing with my mother's death was relatively easy compared to getting on with life without her.

A couple of months had gone by, and I was doing my best to reconnect with a normal life. My sewing machine needed an adjustment, so I drove to the large department store where I had purchased it in downtown Dayton. As I was walking across the immense sales floor, heading to the repair department, I happened upon a demonstration. A group of people was watching a presentation about a new jewelry cleaner. Just as I was about to continue on my way, a woman handed me a small card bearing the number 10. She said that after the presentation, there would be a drawing for a piece of jewelry. I was in a hurry and had a history of never winning anything, but for some reason I stayed. Since the demonstration lasted longer than I expected, though, I picked up my sewing machine and began to continue on my way. I had only taken a few steps when I heard a man yell, "And the winner is . . . number 10!" I was pleasantly surprised that I held the winning number but had no idea what I had won.

The man offered me a small white box in exchange for my number card. Everyone else had left, including the staff doing the demonstration. My heart was bursting with anticipation, and I hoped I would not be disappointed. Upon opening the box, I was astonished to see a gold necklace. I gasped in amazement: the charm hanging from the necklace was a butterfly! I knew this was a gift from my mother, and I did my best to hold back tears.

Six months after my mother's death, my husband accepted a unique job offer, and we relocated our family to Florida. I welcomed the move, which served as a distraction throughout the first year of birthdays and holidays without her. The first anniversary of Mom's death rolled around, and I was the only one who remembered. I purposely did not remind the children or my husband, as I wanted this moment to myself. On July 21, 1988, at 4:30 p.m., I sat in a chair alone on the lanai, facing our in-ground swimming pool. The sun was shining, with a few white, puffy clouds in the sky. I poured a glass of wine and began reminiscing about happy and sad events with my dear mother. At exactly 4:45 p.m., with a tear running down my cheek, I raised my glass and toasted her, saying, "Here's to you, Mom. I love you!" At that exact moment, it began to rain! As the raindrops hit the water in the pool, I knew they were tears from heaven. My mother missed me as much as I missed her.

The rain stopped as quickly as it had come. There wasn't a dark cloud around; the sun had never stopped shining. I ran inside and shared this experience with my husband. While he perceived my experience as part of the grieving process, he did go outside to find that it had not rained on the driveway or in the front yard. With the pool, we really didn't have a backyard. We never spoke of it again.

I didn't dare share this with anyone else, as such things were not openly talked about. This happened thirty-three years ago, and I also securely tucked it away for many years.

My father's second wife, Lucinda (Lou for short), suffered from rheumatoid arthritis. She had a very dominating personality and wanted most things her way. She and my father were avid golfers who loved to travel. Although I tried to get along with Lou, she was a toxic person in my life.

Lou played in a golf league at the country club at which she and my father were members. She was pleased when a new wonder drug came out that took her arthritis pain away: ibuprofen. Taking ibuprofen on a regular basis allowed her many additional years of golfing. What Lou would discover ten years later was that long-term use of ibuprofen can cause chronic kidney disease. Indeed, that was what happened to Lou, at the age of fifty-nine.

By this time we had moved our family back to Ohio. With Lou now on the verge of dialysis and having a strong will to live, she was placed on the kidney transplant list. Faced with the possibility of a terminal illness, she reached out to me, asking for forgiveness for the way that she had treated me over the years. I accepted her apology.

I put up with her overbearing and controlling ways because it was the right thing to do. When she could no longer climb the stairs, I brought over one of our twin beds and helped turn her main floor dining room into a bedroom. When I finished work at my part-time job, I brought her lunch three days a week.

It was only a matter of weeks before Lou received the call that there was a donor match. She was to report to the hospital immediately for a kidney transplant.

The transplant was successful, and she began the regimen of antirejection drug therapy. Out of the hospital and back at home, Lou began a letter of thanks to the family of the person from whom she had received the lifesaving kidney.

It wasn't long before small tumors began appearing randomly. Each time a biopsy was taken, and each time they were benign. What we didn't know was that transplant recipients are three to four times more likely to develop cancer. Another tumor emerged, and another biopsy was performed. This time the results were positive for cancer.

Lou enjoyed spending winters in Key West, Florida, so when the doctor gave her the okay to travel, she and my father booked a flight to search for a house in Key West. She wanted to spend as much time as she could in what she called paradise.

On the day of their flight, I stopped by to say goodbye and pick up their perishables. A friend was taking them to the airport, and I was to pick them up on their return. Lou finished writing down their return flight information and reached out to hand it to me. Something—perhaps a premonition—told me that I would not need the information; I paused and gave her an inquisitive look. She shook the paper and said, "Go on, take it. You are going to be able to pick us up, right?" I accepted the paper, assuring her that I would be picking them up. I knew something was going to happen, but I had no idea what.

Dad and Lou were staying with friends on Big Pine Key. She called once, to let me know they had looked at many houses and should make a decision after checking out a few more. All was good in paradise . . . or so I thought.

It was a Friday night. We had pizza for dinner, opened a bottle of wine, and watched a movie. Feeling relaxed and content, we were getting ready for bed around eleven o'clock, when the phone rang.

"Hello?" I said, in an inquisitive tone since it was rather late.

"Marcia, this is Bev," said the woman with whom Dad and Lou were staying.

Relieved to hear a friendly voice, I said, "Oh, hi, Bev—so good to hear from you. How are you?"

There was a moment of silence, and a bone-tingling chill went up my spine as I asked, "Bev, what's wrong?"

"There has been a car accident. Your dad is in the hospital; he's in critical condition," she said.

"What about Lou?"

"Marcia, I'm sorry to tell you that Lou was killed instantly."

The details were sketchy at that moment. Bev only knew what she had learned from a phone call that she'd made to the police department. "They were house hunting in Key West. We were expecting them for dinner, but they never showed up. We heard on the news about a horrific car accident on the Seven Mile Bridge, so I called the police and explained that our house guests had not shown up for dinner. I gave their names, and the police confirmed that they were involved in the crash."

In a state of shock, I assured Bev that I would book a flight immediately and arrive as soon as I could.

My older brother was living and working in California. He was going to let me assess the situation with our father before flying to Key West himself. I also informed my younger brother, who lived in Vero Beach and had been estranged from Dad for years. He was sorry to hear of the accident but had no desire to rush to his side.

Alone, I arrived at the Key West airport in under twenty-four hours after the fateful phone call. I felt like I carried the weight of the world on my shoulders. Bev and her husband, Eb, picked me up and drove me straight to my father's side.

As I stood outside the hospital, I let the hot breeze embrace my frazzled body. I wanted a whiff of the scent of a vacation, not a health crisis. I knew I had many days of bedside vigil in my future.

I entered my father's room in the ICU. He lay in the bed with tubes in his arms that were hooked up to multiple machines pumping fluids and medications through his veins. His right leg was wrapped, and his limbs were swollen. Surprisingly he was totally aware of the situation. When he saw me, he said, "Honey, Lou is dead."

"I know, Dad. I'm so sorry."

"I need you to take care of her."

"I will, Dad. I will."

"They requested that someone identify the body, and I can't. I need you to do that for me."

"I'll call tomorrow and make the arrangements."

"I want her cremated, and when I'm up to it, we'll have a memorial service."

"How are you doing?"

"Well, I'm alive, but my balls are the size of softballs."

"Gee, thanks for sharing! Do you need a nurse?"

"I've already asked a nurse about it. She said the shock of the injury has to settle somewhere—and lucky me, it is in my balls."

My father may have been critically injured, but he was his old self. I asked if he remembered the accident.

"Yes, I remember what happened, but I can't explain

why it happened," he said, as a tear rolled down his cheek. "We looked at so many houses in Key West, and the day of the accident, we'd finally decided on the one we wanted. Excited, we were driving up the bridge to have dinner with Eb and Bev, when Lou got tired. She reclined her seat and took a power nap while I drove. A few minutes later, a car veered from the opposite lane, crossed the center line and hit us head-on. As the cars collided, the front of each car raised in the air, as if forming the shape of the letter 'A'; then they came crashing back down on the ground. I saw my airbag deploy. It was in the shape of a football and expanded as it came toward my face. Everything seemed to be happening in slow motion. The next thing I remember is looking over at Lou. She was slumped over in the passenger seat; I knew she was dead. I took my hand and rubbed her back, saying goodbye. I knew I was in bad shape. I closed my eyes and waited for the ambulance and police to arrive."

Two days later Eb and Bev drove me to the funeral home to identify Lou's body. We were escorted to the back of the mortuary, where she was lying in a thick cardboard-type box on top of a folding table with wheels. A sheet was drawn up to just under her chin, covering the rest of her body. Since she was to be cremated, minimal makeup and "patchwork" had been done. She was presentable, even though I could see the large dent in her forehead delivered by the dashboard during the accident. How I wished that her children were here; however, she and her daughter had a contentious relationship, and her son was in the military. It was my duty to carry out this identification and blessing for Lou.

Not much of a religious person at that time, I wasn't sure what to do, when suddenly the door opened and in walked the pastor of the local church attended by Dad and Lou while wintering in Key West. Word spreads fast among the locals. The four of us joined hands as the pastor prayed. I felt better signing the document to send Lou's body to the crematorium before requesting a moment alone to say my final farewell.

I sat with my father for weeks, advocating his treatment and care. Trying to save his leg—which the doctor described upon my initial arrival as "hamburger meat"— did happen, but not without surgery to insert a titanium rod to hold the bone together in his upper thigh. Extreme swelling after surgery made it necessary to slice open the outer skin of his leg, loosely wrapping it and hopefully closing the long wound once the swelling had subsided.

During this time Dad was on constant pain medications and began experiencing delusions. One morning he believed he was God. "Good morning, my child," he said.

"Good morning, Dad."

"I'm not Dad. I'm God."

"How are you feeling today?"

"I'm fine, but I need to fix the world."

This type of conversation went on for several days.

In the meantime I spoke to the police about the accident. I requested a copy of the police report, which was personally delivered to me at the hospital by an officer who was honest in his explanation of the incident. "The woman who was driving the car and caused the accident was inadvertently released from jail," he said. "She had been arrested for drugs and was awaiting her arraignment. Paperwork fell through the cracks, and she was released by mistake." He continued, "Upon release she called her boyfriend, asking to borrow his car, and he refused. She knew he kept the keys under the floor mat. She took a taxi to the boyfriend's house and stole the car to procure drugs. She was under the influence of drugs when she swerved from her lane into oncoming traffic, which caused the head-on collision."

The woman had also been seriously injured and was in the same ICU, just two rooms away from my father. I could hear her constantly moaning and yelling out in pain, demanding relief. I complained, and the woman who had killed my stepmother and seriously injured my father was relocated to another floor.

After thirty days of sitting in the hospital, we finally got the okay to hire a medical jet to fly my father from Key West back to Ohio, where he could continue his recovery at home.

I assisted him in his recovery for another six months. During this time I helped him sort through and pack Lou's clothing and belongings until he decided what he wanted to do with them. Lou's favorite perfume was Elizabeth Taylor's White Diamonds. I came home late one night from my father's house with a few of Lou's belongings and decided to display them on my dresser before going to bed. Suddenly I felt a rush of cold wind that blew from the bottom of my feet to the top of my head, leaving behind the scent of her favorite perfume! This was more than a breeze; it was a powerful gust. The fragrance lingered for quite some time. For a few seconds, I could feel her presence. I believed she was letting me know she was okay, and this experience was her final farewell.

My mother had adored my younger brother, Larry. He never missed a celebration with Mom and always placed a bet for her when he attended the Kentucky Derby. I remember when Larry stopped by her house one day, still wearing his softball uniform; she thought he was the most handsome man she had ever seen.

As the middle child between two brothers, I had my own room growing up. My brothers and I were never that close. I remember both of them complaining when they were forced to attend my dance recitals, and I can still hear the constant banging of the drums from when both boys took drum lessons and participated in the high school marching band.

I grew to appreciate Larry when Mom got sick. Larry lived an active life as a single man. He once fell hard for a woman, but it ended in heartbreak, cementing his bachelorhood. When our mother was diagnosed with cancer, the disease progressed quickly. I was nursing her, and it wasn't long until someone had to stay every night. My two young children were in day care. After work my husband cared for them, along with his three children. This was becoming a daunting situation for our family. My older brother cared immensely but was unable to help regularly. Larry came to our assistance, volunteering to come after work and spend the night with Mom every other night so I could go home to be with my family.

During my mother's illness, Larry had a major falling-out with our dad; this was an issue initiated by our father. Larry was so enraged, as our mother, our dad's ex-wife, was on her deathbed, that he broke off contact with everyone in the family, with the exceptions of Mom and me. He stood fast in helping me take care of her.

After Mom's death and the settlement of her small estate, Larry moved to Fort Pierce, Florida. He wanted a fresh start, anywhere but in Ohio. My husband and I would also soon move to Florida, just north of Fort Pierce.

After living in Vero Beach for seven years, another job opportunity brought us back to Ohio. Larry and I kept in touch over the phone.

Several years later Larry was diagnosed with an incurable condition. He didn't share all of the details with me, but I knew it was serious. He was planning to drive to Ohio to stay with us so I could help him through his illness; however, he never made it any further than packing his car. Apparently the pain became so unbearable that he lay on his bed and shot himself in the chest.

Upon receiving the sorrowful and shocking news, Bob and I quickly flew to Vero Beach. With the assistance of my father and his third wife, who just happened to be leaving Naples, Florida, for Ohio, we arranged for two memorial services: one for Larry's Florida friends and the other for friends and family in Ohio. Larry had left me in charge of his estate and all of his belongings. I chose to have him cremated and spread his ashes on the family farm, where Larry had good memories of camping.

After returning to Ohio and completing my executor duties, I was doing my best to return to a normal life, yet again with one fewer family member.

At this time I had several young grandchildren, so I didn't think much of it when I began finding pennies in odd places. I started putting the pennies in a jar, thinking that they belonged to the little ones. I would find a few pennies almost every day—on my nightstand, on the kitchen table, on the bathroom counter, on the floor. It finally dawned on me that the grandkids were not at my house daily, so where were all of those pennies continually coming from? My husband denied leaving pennies around the house. The jar was on the verge of overflowing. I finally searched the internet, finding many articles about something called "pennies from heaven."[2] Deceased loved ones leave pennies, a symbolic reminder that a loved one is watching over you. This explanation brought comfort, and it was something that my younger brother would have done.

In a rush one day, I grabbed my jacket, putting it on as I ran out the door to meet two good friends for lunch. Checking for tissues, I put my hand in one of the jacket pockets . . . to find four pennies! I never put change in my jacket pockets, so I couldn't help but smile as I thought of Larry. I shared the penny story with my friends. They believed it could happen and jokingly suggested that I ask for some silver coins the next time.

That night, before going to bed, I asked out loud for

Larry to leave me some silver coins. When I got up the next morning, I found a small pile of coins in the middle of my placemat on the kitchen table! The pennies were mixed with silver coins! My husband was the only other person in the house, so I asked if he had emptied his pocket and placed coins on the table. He had not. I laughed and smiled and thanked my brother. That was the last time I found any mysterious coins. Larry was very patient waiting for me to figure it out. When I finally perceived the message and he saw me rejoice in remembrance of him, his job was done.

My mind felt like a freshly shaken snow globe. Recalling and acknowledging the signs and messages that I had received over the years was a surreal reawakening.

Now my focus was to pay closer attention and to not be afraid. Participating in ghost hunting has given me a heightened awareness and improved instinctive capabilities. I consider these after-death communications gifts from the other side, and I don't want to miss out on a single one.

Notes

1. Virginia Slims, thin cigarettes produced by Phillip Morris International and marketed to women with the tag line "You've come a long way, baby." https://en.wikipedia.org/wiki/Virginia_Slims
2. Kate Wight, The Cake Library Blog, https://www.joincake.com/blog/finding-pennies-after-someone-dies/

EVIDENCE QUEST

SIX

The Parsonage

It was April 2009, the month in Ohio during which weather and temperatures can dramatically change, sometimes giving us four seasons in a week. It is the month that Bellbrook holds its Sugar Maple Festival,[1] and the weather is always a wondrous surprise.

This day the temperature took an abrupt drop from 64 to 49 degrees. I didn't know if it was the cold breeze or the anticipation of our investigation of my friend Deborah's house causing my excitement.

I was supposed to meet my ghost-hunting friends for the first official investigation of the house she used to use as an office. The last time I had been in this house, something was knocking on the walls. The knocking began softly, almost like the sound of a hushed whisper, and intensified until whoever (or whatever) was knocking received my full attention. Then it all stopped.

As I unlocked the front door, a strange feeling came

over me. It was chillingly silent as I stepped inside, as if the house and I were standing still in time.

"Such a beautiful historic house," I thought as I walked into a small but cozy room. The room was adorned with crown molding; a built-in bookcase stood tall, next to the vintage fireplace that was detailed with custom wooden headers under a quaint mantel, all painted white. The owner certainly had a true passion for decorating to match the story and past of the house.

The house, which was believed to be haunted, didn't exhibit any commonplace antics associated with otherworldly activity. I sat on the couch and listened to the silence. I found that the quieter the room, the more I could hear—things I did not notice before.

The brief moment of tranquility quickly came to an end, as I heard conversations, footsteps, and the rustling of plastic bags on the front porch. My ghost-hunting friends were here. Dave Jones, John Brown, and Kristin Ginett came through the door. They had been across the street at the gas station stocking up on drinks and snacks, as they planned on staying well into the night. I was the keeper of the key and was responsible for locking up, which meant a late night for me, as well.

Dave and John set up two night vision camcorders upstairs, and everyone had their digital recorders running. I was downstairs, sitting in the cozy room on the settee, while everyone else was upstairs. I had been on several ghost investigations with these people, listening to EVPs that they had captured, yet I still wasn't totally convinced it was that easy. While they were upstairs doing their thing,

I opened my purse and retrieved my very first piece of ghost-hunting equipment: my own digital recorder. I had no plan of asking any questions. I simply turned it on and set it on the mantel.

I eventually joined the group upstairs. Shortly afterward Dave listened to his digital recorder and was excited to share an EVP that he had captured. It was a woman who sounded like she was from the time of the Underground Railroad, a secret escape network during the era of slavery. A female voice could be heard saying, "Ya got to he'p me now, ya hear?" Dave thought that she may have been a slave hoping to make it to safety. Fugitive slaves were Black (or African American), and since John was Black, the rest of the group asked him to do an EVP session in the cellar, a common place for slaves to hide.

The trap door–style entrance to the cellar was located in the floor of the former butler's pantry. The small area of the cellar now housed the furnace. The walls were made of the original stone foundation, with a very tiny window on one side. I decided to follow John into the cellar while he did his EVP session. For safety's sake I felt it best that nobody did such things alone.

John went down first, a recorder and flashlight in hand. As I was carefully descending the narrow cement steps, he suddenly yelled, "Oh, shit!"

Immediately spooked, I said, "What's wrong?"

Brushing off his sleeve, he replied, "Oh, it's a dead spider!" Thankfully it was dark, so he could not see me smiling, trying my best to hold back laughter. As I took my place by his side, he whispered, "I really hate spiders."

John shined his flashlight all around the cellar. A couple old doors were stored there. This wasn't a hidden room, by any means, and there was no sign of an old tunnel. The Underground Railroad was actually a network of people and places that formed an escape route to escort slaves to freedom; however, several buildings in this area once had underground tunnels connecting houses to their barns.

I stood quietly while John conducted his EVP session.

Approximately thirty minutes later, John and I emerged from the cellar and headed upstairs, to find Dave lying on the floor asleep and Kristin sitting on the floor, leaning against a wall. Dave's camcorder was taped to the doorframe near the floor, pointing into the small room set up as a nursery—the same room in which the owners had found a dozen shells removed from the chair rails and neatly stacked on the floor. It was nearing two o'clock in the morning, and John and I also sat down.

A few minutes later, we heard an odd noise. It was a short series of sounds similar to bandages being ripped off. Suddenly the camcorder flung itself from the doorjamb, hitting the sleeping Dave in the head! Dave jumped up, discovering that the adhesive on the duct tape he used had come loose. I think the ghosts were laughing at us that night.

Dave stayed upstairs while the rest of us headed down to gather our belongings. By happenstance, Kristin, John, and I were standing in a straight line between the front room and living room entrances, about four feet from one another. Without warning we heard the laughter of a little girl. It passed by Kristin first, who turned her head from left to right, naturally following the sound. As it passed by John, he instinctively did the same thing; then, after passing by me, the sound turned and went upstairs. The girl's laughter was quite loud and jovial. I had no idea what I had just experienced. John explained that it was a disembodied voice: a voice that we hear with our own ears but can't see the source of. It's a voice without a body, unlike an EVP (which can only be heard upon playback). I was amazed and truly wondering if the ghost was laughing with us or at us! Had that tape come undone on its own?

Under the guidance of Dave and John, I learned how to upload the audio from my digital recorder into an editing program that would allow me to make clips, should I actually hear something other than our own conversations. I was wearing a cheap pair of headphones that I used for quick sound checks when setting up my video camera at events. They were lightweight and originally had a layer of foam rubber over the earpieces, but one of my cats had chewed the foam off.

Listening to and reliving an investigation was not the same as being there. Since my recorder was downstairs and the investigation was upstairs, I heard only muffled conversations from above, with the sounds of my own breathing and the occasional cough or stomach growl.

After over an hour of listening, I was completely bored. I was at the point on the recording at which I had joined the others upstairs. I could hear my footsteps growing fainter in the distance, when I heard something.

"What was that?" I said to myself.

Stopping the playback and going back thirty seconds, I heard it again. There were definitely a few spoken words! I turned up the volume and played it back again, and there it was—plain as day, a female voice, saying, "What's she doing?" To my amazement I had actually captured an unidentified voice intelligently responding to my actions. Spirit was wondering what I was doing as I headed upstairs.

It was official: I had captured my first EVP! If I could have, I would have done cartwheels. I couldn't care less about pseudoscience or human perception. I had no desire to try to explain to anyone that spirit energy may possibly be able to alter static noise to sound like a human voice to be able to communicate with us. The fact was that I had collected my first EVP, and I'd come by it honestly. Sure, EVPs can easily be faked, but I was a person of integrity, so when I shared this with my newly founded paranormal support group, they did not doubt me one bit.

Dave and John were happy for me. They told me the stories of their first EVPs. It is a monumental step in this research field.

The first thing I did was invest in a pair of good headphones. I had spent $50 on my digital recorder, now I chose a pair of Bose headphones on sale for $150. I felt that I was officially a ghost hunter.

We all met at the house, formerly a parsonage, with Deborah, to update her on the results of the investigation.

We laughed when John showed the video clip from his camcorder, capturing Dave's camera coming loose and scaring him awake. Dave shared more EVPs. John had caught an EVP of a racial slur while in the cellar. John was experimenting with a duo recording technique that gave him stellar results. All of us, as ghost hunters, dubbed the parsonage officially "haunted."

Deborah graciously let us back into the house on future occasions for additional investigations and local events. She supported my events wholeheartedly.

$\smile$

I will never forget another investigation at the parsonage. I was now a seasoned paranormal researcher and had drawn more people into my band of provisional investigators. I knew the location and history of the parsonage were key to its paranormal activity. The energy in this house was intense, but I was not afraid. I felt that the spirits, or ghosts, were interacting with me and my friends for a reason. I was in the midst of my own journey, and I did not yet know the outcome. While many of my friends were having fun, I took what I was doing very seriously.

I had acquired a new wireless mini digital video recorder (DVR) system. My DVR, an electronic device that records video in a digital format, recorded to a secure digital (SD) memory card. After setting the DVR monitor downstairs in the parsonage living room and placing a camera upstairs in the open area on the second floor, I welcomed a local couple, Jan Berryhill and her husband, who had attended many ghost hunts with me and the ghost-hunting team. I believe having local people on ghost hunts is beneficial in getting results.

As we sat in the open area on the second floor, a sudden, short-lived thunderstorm took place. I had one of the locals hold dowsing rods. Sitting on the floor, holding his arms as still as possible, he began asking questions. The rods were moving as requested, seemingly in response to his questions. When his arms tired, we moved him into a chair in the back bedroom (the one connected to the nursery room), where he could rest his arms as he held the rods. Stationing someone downstairs to watch the DVR monitor, I moved the DVR camera into that room, pointing at him. The camera view included the door that opened into the middle area.

The storm passed. Darkness began to fall, and the camera went into night vision mode. The local man began talking to friends and former neighbors who were now deceased. The rods crossed and uncrossed on command to his questions.

Suddenly the woman stationed downstairs began screaming. "Oh my God!" she exclaimed.

"What? What do you see?" I asked, yelling so that I could be heard downstairs.

"Orbs! Orbs are everywhere!" she said. "I've never seen anything like it!"

Orbs (spherical bodies of light) are another subject, which I will address soon enough. What you need to know for now is that if you don't believe in orbs, you need to believe in orbs in Bellbrook.

When I reviewed the DVR footage, I was amazed to see a phenomenon that I've never witnessed before. It literally looked like it was snowing orbs inside the second floor of that house—orbs in all varying degrees of size and intensity. They were falling from the ceiling to the floor—some going sideways, both from the left and from the right. There were no fans, no open windows. They were going up and going down. All the while the dowsing rods were constantly moving, and the local man was calling out names of known deceased people from the community. It was a sight to behold, and my gut feeling was to say thank you. It was an incredibly enchanting moment for me. I left the parsonage that night with a feeling of euphoria.

Notes

1. Sugar Maple Festival, Bellbrook, Ohio. https://www.sugarmaplef-estival.com

SEVEN

The Marshall House

It was a warm evening in August when I joined six other ghost hunters to investigate a 2,750-square-foot home that sat on over two acres in Sugarcreek Township, Ohio. The old historical house that once prominently stood on a one-thousand-acre homestead still stands, amid so much change.

A veteran of the War of 1812, John Marshall[1] built the stately two-story farmhouse in 1837, most likely without the five eighteen-foot porch columns the house sports today.

The nearly two-hundred-year-old house, now standing on only two acres, concealed a secret tunnel in the cellar that led to the barn.[2] This property has since been documented as part of the Underground Railroad. Although the original barn now lies in a pile of rubble, still standing are a springhouse and a large building that housed the chicken coop.

John Marshall came to Ohio from Kentucky at the age

of nineteen and secured a patent to a tract of one thousand acres of wilderness land along the banks of the Little Miami River, at a time when land with its own water supply was very important. Shortly after that John married Sara, and together they built a log cabin by the river. They lived there until their new house was ready to occupy.

The once proud and mighty mansion was badly in need of improvements when the current owners purchased it. Together they tackled the renovations, bringing it back to life, bit by bit restoring the house to its original splendor.

Going into this investigation, I was more of a believer in ghosts than a skeptic; however, the scientific side of me still wanted evidence. To better capture potential evidence, I needed a good camcorder with night vision. I ordered a Canon XA10 Professional Camcorder with 64GB internal memory and two SDXC compatible memory card slots. This would allow for hours of video recording. It was designed for situations in which mobility was critical while shooting. This made it perfect for ghost-hunting. My paranormal investigating tools also included a digital electromagnetic field (EMF) meter that could detect natural and human-made EMF frequencies and ambient temperature changes, as well as a meter using sound, light and needle activity. Three Mini Maglite flashlights of different colors were also staples in my tool kit. At this time my investment in equipment was just over $2,500. I was very dedicated in this venture.

The current owner explained that one of the latest families to reside in the home before him raised twin girls, both alive at the time of this investigation, one of whom now lived across the street in a newer housing development. He and others occasionally felt a cool breeze rush by from one of the bedrooms and continue down the stairs. The bedroom in question was the room in which the twin girls had been raised.

My camcorder was set up in the upstairs hall, near that bedroom and the hall window. Dave Jones, with whom I'd been on several investigations by this time, remained in the bedroom, doing EVP work with his digital recorder. I decided to join two other investigators in the cellar, while the rest went to investigate the outbuildings.

The kitchen afforded easy access to the cellar. I slowly descended into the dark cellar with investigators Lee and Patti Allen.

The once dirt floor was now concrete, with the exception of a corner area in the back, where the entrance to the underground tunnel had been.

The stone foundation appeared to be in good shape, still holding the original structure after almost two hundred years. The cellar had three defined spaces, the largest of which appeared to be used for storage. A smaller room in the back, sectioned off by a stone archway, had most likely been used as a root cellar in the early days. The corner with the dirt floor connected to the smaller room. It did not appear to have been a coal or wood cellar, since its few windows were too small to accommodate any type of delivery wagon. I noticed the windows were too little for anyone to crawl through, and I duly noted to myself that the only way out of this cellar was from the door through which we had entered. If escape would be necessary, it would be unlikely, now that the tunnel had been filled in. I knew it would certainly be dark in the cellar when the lights were turned off. At this time I was still relatively new to the paranormal investigation field, and I didn't think to bring anything with me or even grab a flashlight I had in my equipment bag. I was still a bit intimidated, and I'll admit that I was a little spooked about looking for ghosts. The overhead light was turned off, and then Lee also turned off his flashlight. Instantaneous darkness hit me in the face. I felt my heart rate surge, and I did my best to keep my cool. In a few short moments, my eyes better adjusted to the dark, as my position allowed me to see the small window in the back room (where, thankfully, moonlight was shining in).

Lee began an EVP session as he held a digital recorder. During the session something would occasionally block part of the window in my field of vision. The three of us were in the large room, facing the smaller room. I think my heart skipped a beat at the realization that if something was blocking the moonlight, whatever it was had to be between us and the window! Before I could say anything, someone said, "There is a shadow person in the small room. Do you see it?" All three of us confirmed that we saw something. Now directly focused on the archway into the small room, I saw a dark figure lean into the open doorway, as if looking to see what we were doing. When it leaned in, the moonlight created a backdrop. I could see the shape of shoulders and a head, then it retreated behind the stone wall. This occurred about three times before the other two ghost hunters decided to enter the small room.

I was slightly terrified to knowingly walk into a room in which I had just seen something that I could not explain. This was not the first time I had seen a shadow of a person, not dependent on the sun's light. While I managed to stay calm, there was no way I was going to stand in the large room alone with no phone, camera, or flashlight.

I was the second one to enter the small room. To my surprise, nothing was there. The room was brighter, being so close to the moonlit window. While the others continued their EVP session, I was planning an escape route should the necessity arrise. I managed to station myself by the open archway so I would be the first one out; then we all heard what sounded like a female whimpering in the corner, where the tunnel used to be, followed by what sounded like small stones being crushed underfoot and heavy footsteps approaching the small room. There was a pause . . . and then the footsteps continued, sounding as if they were coming even closer! Lee made his way past me, saying, "It sounds like a man wearing boots." I was happy to change places with him.

It was my thought that John Marshall was an abolitionist. Another investigator felt that he may have mistreated a slave, hence the female whimpering in the corner. Lee began antagonizing the mysterious "walker." "Who do you think you are?" he goaded. "I don't like what you did!" Just then we noticed that the room grew darker; it was like a curtain of darkness descended over us. We could not see the moonlight anymore; we could not see our hands in front of our faces.

We decided it would be a positive gesture to sing a spiritual song that the slaves used to sing, but as none of us knew one, we opted to sing the hymn "Amazing Grace." I was a bit more embarrassed than scared to sing in my off-key baritone voice, but I was the only one who knew the words. Lee hummed the tune, as my crackling, unharmonious vocal cords belted out "Amazing grace, how sweet the sound ..." It wasn't a sweet sound, by any means, but by the time we reached the end of the song, the darkness had lifted, and I was relieved.

Lee turned on his flashlight, and we ended the session. I could not wait to return upstairs to the kitchen, where we had stored our equipment bags. The first thing I did was grab a flashlight and my small digital camera.

Upon returning from the cellar, I realized a quick rain shower had ensued, making the cellar darker when the gloomy clouds passed through. We had no idea at the time that this had occurred.

Now feeling safe, I joined the other investigators in the bedroom on the second floor that had the noted activity of a cool passing breeze. When I had set up my camcorder in the upstairs hallway before going down to the cellar, the windows were open, because it was a warm evening. I decided to review the footage before attaching a newly charged battery pack.

To my amazement the camcorder had documented a small, round anomaly suddenly appear in the bottom section of the open window on the second floor. It hovered for a couple seconds, steadily rotated three times and then vanished! The anomaly appeared in the area of the window screen, eliminating this as a reflection on the glass. Nobody I was investigating with had ever seen something like this before.

As I began my second investigation session, Dave reported picking up a woman's name, Edna, during an EVP session. The homeowner had provided us with a binder with the history of the house, and Dave found that there were two women named Edna who had resided in the house at different times. One of the investigators experienced the reported "breeze" leaving that bedroom, and light, quick footsteps were picked up on the recorder. They believed it was Edna Cramer, the woman who raised her twins there. Possibly she was rushing to the kitchen to get something that the twins needed. It was also noted that Edna passed away of old age in that particular bedroom.

The time was nearing one thirty in the morning, and the homeowner requested that we wrap up the investigation by two o'clock. Lee, Patti, and Jim Wilson (another investigator) went upstairs to check the bedroom. They had an EMF meter that also registered temperature changes. Lee asked if Patti was silly, and the meter sounded off one time. Everyone laughed, and then Lee asked the spirit, "Are you silly?" The meter went off like crazy, making electronic tones, to the point that Jim asked the spirit to please back away from the device. At the foot of the metal bed frame, the heat sensor went off. Jim backed away from the bed, wondering if he should reset the meter . . . which suddenly reset itself! The meter began making sounds. Although a bit off-key (like my singing in the cellar), they were recognizable as "Amazing Grace." It was copying my singing!

After that we were in the kitchen, packing up our cameras and equipment, when we realized that one investigator, Jon Greene, was missing. The homeowner walked through the house and found him asleep in a chair in an upstairs bedroom. Lee grabbed my digital camera, which recorded video, while Dave quickly retrieved a whistle from his equipment bag. The men giggled quietly as they went upstairs. The rest of us, including the homeowner, remained in the kitchen. We heard Dave blow his whistle loudly, startling Jon out of his sleep, while Lee recorded it. Then we heard a roar of laughter.

As Dave packed his whistle away, Lee asked me to replay the movie. Afterward, as I put my camera inside its case, we all heard a loud and resounding whistle coming from upstairs, but nobody was up there! The homeowner was surprised, confirming that he heard it too.

After some discussion Dave explained that he felt the ghost in the house had an interactive personality, possibly retaining its temperament from when it was alive. We all agreed that this ghost enjoyed jesting banter and letting us know it was around by copying some of the things that we did that night. It was an amazing way to end the investigation of this beautiful and historic house.

Notes

1. G.F. Robinson, *History of Greene County, Ohio.*
2. History and documentation from the owners.

EIGHT

The Bellbrook Historical Museum

American historic house museums are in abundance; there is one in just about every city in the United States. These museums are usually located in former private homes of wealthy locals, either donated or acquired by not-for-profit organizations or the towns' historical societies.

In Bellbrook, Ohio, at the corner of North Main and Walnut streets, the Bellbrook Historical Museum is a place that will take you beyond its walls to learn about Bellbrook's history. It will show you how things have (or haven't) changed in this historic little town.

The building that houses the museum was an old pioneer home of log construction, circa 1825. While clapboard siding now covers the squared logs, the museum has left a small section unsided, so the original structure can be viewed under an acrylic sheet.

In 1965, the house was graciously donated to the (then) Village of Bellbrook by Evelyn Brock Deger (1894–1977), specifically to be used as a historical museum.[1] A board of trustees appointed by a city council manages the museum. (Bellbrook achieved city status in 1974.)

Evelyn was one of the Bellbrook area's best known citizens. She also donated the land for a park in the heart of town, which was named Bellbrock park in honor of her.

One showcased exhibit is a black oak high-back bench hand carved by Bellbrook's own Della Hopkins Knox (1870–1957) in 1900. Della, a self-taught wood carver, used a pen knife (small folding knife) to carve the intricate details on the large bench. Della studied art at the Dermot School for Young Ladies in Xenia, Ohio, while living in Bellbrook. In 1886, she enrolled in the Art Academy in Cincinnati, later earning a Master of Arts degree from Columbia University in New York. Della taught art for most of her life. Another masterpiece of Della's, an oil painting titled "Portrait of a Girl," also known as "The Picture of a Porage Girl" (recently restored), proudly hangs in the museum.

The museum's most unusual ghostly phenomenon was unexplained footsteps. After volunteers told me that they heard footsteps on the second floor of the museum while alone on the first floor, I was granted permission to investigate. In June 2009, I once again joined Dave Jones' team of investigators. It was a warm evening, and it began to rain as the president of the museum trustees arrived to unlock the door. He graciously said that he would give us until midnight, when he would return to lock up.

Entrusting my friends and me with the treasures in the museum was indeed an honor, which I did not take lightly. Once inside, being mindful of the velvet rope dividing the living room from the hall, I found it quiet and peaceful. Digital recorders were running, and many photos were taken.

Three of us ventured to the landing on the second floor. The second-story bedrooms were set up with displays of antique artifacts, including quilts, toys, and a wooden bed strung with rope that supported the mattress, usually stuffed with straw. After standing there for approximately ten minutes, two of us got dizzy, and I momentarily lost my balance. One man felt nauseated, prompting us to return to the first floor. I noted the landing was slightly slanted, which may have accounted for me losing my balance, but we could not explain what made us dizzy and one man feel sick.

When the rain stopped, we went outside to walk around the building and take photos. We noticed that near the corner of the house where we had become dizzy, an electric pole stood. Multiple conductor wires, as well as a streetlight and what may have been cable or telephone lines, were hung about the same height as the second-floor ceiling. These wires most likely carried high- and low-voltage electricity for use by customers and probably caused our dizziness and illness. Power lines can create a type of electronic pollution, which can bring on feelings of nausea and dizzy spells.

Back inside, Dave set up a static device that used LED lights, activated when an electrical charge (a charged object) came into contact with the mechanism. The static device was sitting on a table near the stairway, not far from the front door. Those of us monitoring this device were at minimum six feet away.

Since it was a warm summer night and it had rained most of the evening, there was moisture in the air, which isn't conducive to objects holding static charges well. We were engaged in conversation, not expecting the device to light up . . . when it suddenly did. Dave asked out loud if there was more than one spirit in the museum, and the light on the device turned on again. Unfortunately that was the only other time the device reacted.

The Crowl undertaker building, located on the museum grounds, was donated by Mr. and Mrs. Rex Black in 1979.[2] The display is behind a glass enclosure, and a motion detector starts an audio program when the door is opened. Investigating this area brought no experience or evidence of any kind.

Not long after the investigation, one of the new trustees of the museum also told me that she had heard noises and footsteps in the museum as she worked in the enclosed office area alone. I volunteered to train as a docent, and I met with her one afternoon to interview her for a newspaper article that I had agreed to write.

We first walked through both floors of the museum as she pointed out a few things that had been added to the display. Nobody was in the museum, so we settled into the office and began the interview. All was going well when we both heard what sounded like a rock being thrown onto the wood floor in the room next to the office. The trustee was noticeably alarmed. I motioned for her to be quiet. We waited and heard the noise again, this time closer to the office door. Excited, I walked into the other room, with the trustee following right behind. We found no evidence of anything that could have made the noise. Just then we both heard three footsteps walking across the floor upstairs. I quickly went upstairs to find nothing, but it was something to experience exactly what the volunteers had.

Notes

1. Bellbrook Historical Museum, Bellbrook Historical Society FB page and City of Bellbrook website. http://www.cityofbell-brook.org/page/community_museum, https://www.facebook.com/pages/category/Community/Bellbrook-Sugarcreek-His-torical-Society-186200064787298/, http://www.cityofbell-brook.org

2. Bellbrook Historical Museum, Bellbrook Historical Society and City of Bellbrook website.

NINE

The Bellbrook Presbyterian Church

One of the most beautiful small, historic churches in Bellbrook quietly sits in the northwest quadrant of the Old Village, taking you on a spiritual journey through history.

The current Bellbrook Presbyterian Church was built in 1890, although the church was organized in 1828.

The first church building was constructed in 1829, on a hill west of the village. Members who walked from the village crossed the Little Sugarcreek river on a log footbridge to reach it. The congregation worshipped in this building until 1858, when they bought from the Universalists a church that stood on the present site.

This church was made of frame construction with a steeple that housed a bell. Being the only church in town to have a bell, it was known as the "bell church." The building was moved to North West Street, where it served as a barn, housing a hearse and other undertaking equipment of W. H. Morris. It burned in 1895.[1]

The new church, a red brick structure now 132 years

old, sits on a limestone foundation, common in western Ohio in the 1800s. The bell tower stands taller than the rest of the building. The openings in the belfry, which allow the sound to escape, are trimmed with wood louvers. The double doors in the front are adorned with a semicircular stained glass window in shades of blue, and the brick was laid to create a grand arched entryway. High above the entrance, the brick wall features a circular stained glass window—some call it the Rose Window—with hues of green and orange and a blue five-point star in the center. High on the back brick wall, where classrooms were added in 1955 and 1964, a large, circular gable vent was constructed with wooden slats. Entering this building is like taking a step back in time.

On July 1, 2011, seven of us investigated the church, 121 years old at the time. It isn't easy for a paranormal group to be granted permission to investigate an active house of worship, but a friend of mine was an elder of the church who trusted my integrity and the people with whom I held a common bond.

We parked behind the building. We had been told about the presence of bats in the upper areas of the church, which made me wonder if this is how the phrase "bats in the belfry" (which actually means that someone isn't all there in the head) was coined. We arrived before dark, as we wanted to experience the bats leaving their roost; this is common on warm nights, so they can find food and water. We gathered our equipment, and as the sun was setting and darkness began to fall, bats started flying out from between the wooden slats on the gable vent—first just a few, then they emerged by the tens, and suddenly it was like a blanket of black soaring into the sky by the hundreds! What an incredible sight! The elders were in the process of hiring a professional to develop a humane bat removal strategy, as a long-term health hazard from bat droppings was facing them.

We entered the building through the back door, which led directly into the kitchen and serving area. There was a seating section and a hallway that led to the classroom area, one large room that could be sectioned off by dividers. Another room housed a nursery.

We entered the front of the sanctuary, referred to as the chancel. In the chancel was the Communion table. A gold cross sat in the middle of the table behind the Bible and stand, between two candles. On this day a gold-fringed Communion cloth covered the top of the table.

On the arched wall of the chancel hung red curtains and a large wooden cross. The pulpit, a podium for the pastor, was located to the left of the Communion table. Two small balcony-style boxes high up on both sides of the chancel held large pipes that used to be connected to a pipe organ. A piano sat on the opposite side of the pulpit, but I did not see any evidence of an organ.

A slightly worn red carpet ran throughout the church. The padded seats on the wooden pews almost matched the carpet. Three large, arched stained-glass windows adorned each side, enhancing the beauty of this small, historic church.

I set up my camcorder on a small tabletop tripod on the back edge of the Communion table, so it overlooked the entire seating area of the church. Others were running digital recorders; Dave wore headphones connected to his digital recorder, listening for live EVPs. I found this interesting, as I always discovered EVPs on my recorder after the investigation was over. To date I have never heard a live EVP. I decided this time to try it myself. My camcorder was turned on but not yet recording. As another investigator called me to the classrooms in the back, I explained to John and Dave how to start the video recording.

The other investigator (and church elder), Andrew Berryhill, was using my EMF meter. Some investigators had made fun of the marketing of the device, which said that in certain modes recent ghosts appeared every three to five minutes, while ancient ghosts appeared every seven to fifteen minutes. The manufacturer compares this capability to human thoughts as they travel infinitely through space and become paranormal energies. I didn't need this device to detect the possible powers of a conscious universe; I just needed to look for EMF in the back room.

In "gauss" mode, the EMF meter looked for EMF fields (low and radio frequency); the meter's needle would move and the device blink a red light when an EMF was detected. Gauss is the unit of measurement of magnetic flux density, which is the amount of the magnetic field in a particular area.

Andrew had completed an EMF scan of the large classroom and found it strange that there was no EMF near the walls of the room; however, there was an EMF in the middle of the room that spanned approximately ten feet long and three feet wide above an area of folding tables and chairs. The meter did not react a foot above or below the area. It was like an EMF cloud simply hovered in that spot. Electric outlets in the walls did not affect the meter. Light fixtures in the ceiling, with lights turned off, did not set off the meter either. Andrew wanted another person to witness the finding, so I began snapping photos, with nothing showing up in any of them. I wished I had a compass, so we could measure the direction of the magnetic field. I knew that magnetic fields occur whenever charge is in motion; this is what sets off our static devices. This magnetic field, however, was not moving.

With the investigation in full swing, I returned to the chancel area to find John excited about a light blue anomaly that had appeared near the ceiling of the church. He said that it appeared and hovered for just a few seconds before disappearing. John was sure the camcorder had picked it up. Eager to check it out, I went to review the camcorder footage, only to find that the camcorder was not recording. I guess John thought Dave had hit the record button, and Dave thought John had. It happens. Now that the dark of night was upon us, I switched the camcorder into infrared mode and pushed the record button myself.

I sat on the front pew of the center section, while Dave quietly walked the aisles conducting an EVP session. Andrew, Patrick, and John sat in pews on the left. The lights were off, with the exception of exit signs and one electric candle flickering on the back windowsill. It was quiet and peaceful in the dark little church while our equipment was busy recording.

About an hour into this session, the motion light outside the door near the chancel turned on. A minute later it turned off. Andrew asked, "If anyone is outside the church near the door, please turn the light on again." A few seconds later, the light turned on. Andrew got up and quickly walked to the door, to find a cat wandering around the area. Before returning, he checked to see if the EMF field was still present in the large classroom. It was.

After two hours of sitting in the church in the depths of silence, suddenly a loud growling sound pierced the stillness. Patrick jumped up and exclaimed, "Did you hear that? It sounded like a disembodied voice!"

As Patrick and Dave began to rewind their digital recorders to play back the sound, I embarrassedly stood up and said, "Sorry, but that was my stomach growling!"

The guys were disappointed but laughing. You see, there is nothing in the stomach to muffle such sounds, and when you are in a soundless environment, it is quite noticeable. I realized that this may be why the others brought snacks with them to every investigation. It was after midnight, and I was hungry.

Andrew and I returned to the classroom where the EMF was earlier detected to find that the field was gone. A quick review of some of the camcorder footage showed something flying near the floor, in front of the pew in which I was sitting. It appeared bright white, which is normal for infrared camera footage. Going frame by frame, it appeared to have wings. Although it would have been great to have a small angelic figure visiting us, it was flying in circles, as insects tend to do to keep themselves aligned with a light source. We deemed the anomaly a bug.

The church elder asked that we wrap up the investigation in an hour. He was responsible for locking the building, and he was getting tired, as we were nearing two o'clock.

We gathered in the nursery, where one investigator turned on a P-SB7 spirit box attached to an external speaker. The spirit box (or what we call the ghost box) is a device that provides real-time responses. It has a millisecond adjustable forward and reverse frequency sweep that creates a high frequency white noise as it scans through AM or FM channels, allowing spirits to communicate through the white noise generated by these frequencies.

We elected one person to ask the questions during the ghost box session. Communication started almost immediately, with the question of "What town are we in?" During the sweep the first syllable of the town came through: "Bell." Immediately the next channel said, "Brook" . . . Bellbrook! We were all amazed. The next question was "What type of building are we in?" The word "church" came through the ghost box. The answers began coming in multiple words, which hasn't been the norm for the ghost box sessions that I've been in. For almost half an hour, our questions were answered with verifiable information.

One person wondered if we were hearing words from random radio stations. I figured the odds of multiple words coming through a millisecond scan of frequencies that actually made sense were pretty extreme. There had been some geeks out there who actually created a simulated spirit box, using a programming language, a phonetic dictionary, and code. To get into a few of the nerdy details, they cross-referenced their dictionary with a list of the one thousand most common words. They used an approximate time of thirty seconds per spirit box sample, assuming that most words discovered would be three phonemes long. If twelve phonemes fit into one second, they could hear up to 120 words in thirty seconds; however, they only heard three words on average. They determined that there was a 0.38 percent chance of hearing two words in a row. Their further study found that there was a 0.01 percent chance of hearing three words in a row (which we did during our ghost box session). According to their findings, this was statistically significant and was not likely to occur randomly.[2]

It should be noted this experiment was performed by two nonbelievers of ghosts but big believers in statistics.

We were never sure whom we were talking to through the ghost box, but at this point it didn't matter. Having this experience of a possible real-time conversation with someone from the other side was amazing for all of us.

Notes

1. *Sesquicentennial Program and History,* June 1966.
2. Ashley Villar and Alex McCarthy, *The Statistics of Spirit Boxes.* https://medium.com/@astrovav/the-statistics-of-spirit-boxes-2cf021bf6c3

CHAPTER TEN

The Gebhart House

Sometimes a paranormal investigation leads to uncovering secrets and, in some cases, crimes, as you begin to explore and research the history of a residence or business. This was the case for a house in Bellbrook's Old Village area. What began as a generic investigation as a favor to me from a realtor friend turned into a discovery of possible criminal activity and suicide.

In October 2012, as the sun began to set, I found myself keying in the code (entrusted to me) to a lockbox securing the 112-year-old traditional two-story frame home belonging to my friend; however, the code didn't seem to be working. I realized the lockbox wasn't locked. It had been left open, which put the all-woman investigation team on edge.

Having found myself in compromising situations on prior investigations, we phoned the father of one of the investigators, who lived nearby, to come into the house with us.

After checking every room on the first and second

floors and finding no one, we ventured into the basement, where we were astonished to see what appeared to be the aftermath of a crime. As we stood on the wooden staircase, remnants of the foundation of a false wall were just two feet away. Part of the fake wall remained standing further out, while splintered pieces of wood were scattered about. There was a hidden walkway behind the false wall, leading to a concealed part of the basement in which a wood slat door opened to another door covered in carpet. It appeared the hardware that once secured both doors had been hastily removed.

As my heart skipped a beat, the man helping us said that he recalled the former owners of the house building what they called a safe room, in hope of surviving any "Year 2000" computer issues. (There was great fear of a "Y2K bug" at the turn of the century, a computer glitch dealing with dates beyond December 31, 1999. It was thought that it could cause pandemonium among the nation's power, communications, and financial systems, all of which were connected by computers.)

As a mother, seeing the carpeted door hidden behind a wooden door (that used to have outside locks) enclosed by a false wall made me quite apprehensive.

One of my colleagues opened the door that led into the secret room. She stepped inside, finding a light switch that still operated one fluorescent light hanging from the ceiling. The inside of the room was also carpeted: floor, walls, and ceiling. At one end was a wooden bench with a round hole in the middle where a bucket could fit underneath, creating a makeshift toilet. A pillow and blanket lay folded at the other end. The room was no more than four feet wide and eight feet tall. This appeared to be a place in which to confine someone against their will.

While I peeked in, I could not step inside; I was sick to my stomach imagining what may have, or could have, happened within.

In a small town, neighbors are aware of strangers among them; however, I was known well enough in the town that the people who lived in the surrounding residences eagerly approached me. I was told that their neighbor, Randy Gebhart, had committed suicide in his upstairs bedroom ten years earlier. After talking to several neighbors, who put me in contact with one of Randy's former coworkers, I discovered that Randy had been accused of attempting to lure young girls into his house. After procuring a copy of the police report, I uncovered the official charge of criminal child enticement. (A person commits a crime of enticement of a child if he or she invites or persuades, or attempts to persuade, a child under the age of fifteen years to enter any vehicle, building, room, or secluded place with the intent to commit sexual assault or unlawful sexual contact upon said child.)

According to personal interviews that I conducted with neighbors and an internet search of public records, Randy Gebhart attempted to entice several twelve-year-old girls into his home to take their pictures. The girls ran home and told their parents. One of these girls was Randy's niece; her mother (Randy's sister) called the police. It should be noted that her boyfriend at the time was a police officer for another jurisdiction.

I spoke with Randy's coworker at a local electric company, who revealed that he officially requested to be reassigned work partners because Randy was making inappropriate comments about the young daughter of a couple with whom the coworker was residing. The request was granted.

According to the police report, Randy's arraignment was held in August in the early 2000s, during which he pleaded not guilty. The court ordered a no contact order for three young girls, including his niece, and all other minors, with the exception of his own two children.

During my continuing interviews, several neighbors recalled seeing Randy driving a van down the street where his home was located after his arraignment. He was visibly upset, and his face was red. That was the last time those neighbors saw Randy Gebhart alive.

Another police report said that a neighbor (Randy's brother) requested a "welfare check" on Randy Gebhart. The same neighbor called the police a second time, saying that he had put a ladder to the second-floor window and had seen a man lying on the bed. He wasn't sure if he was breathing or maybe just sleeping.

Police entered the house and found Randy lying on his back with a pillow over his face, with blood on the bed and floor. It appeared that Randy had shot himself in the head with an Astra .25-caliber pistol. The gun had one bullet in the chamber and four in the clip. The fired casing was stuck to the pillow next to Randy's head. By this time a dozen family members of Randy's had gathered outside the house.

Neighbors heard that he left a suicide note. The police report confirmed that the decedent's last will and testament lay on a table across the room from the bed. The investigation ruled Randy's death a suicide.

We were granted another entrance into this house to complete our investigation attempt two weeks later.

I set up my Canon XA10 camcorder in the bedroom in which Randy Gebhart took his own life. I also set up a DVR camera in the basement, with the monitor on the first floor. Digital recorders were placed on all three floors. In addition we used a handheld camcorder, and a digital EMF device was on to monitor any EMF spikes.

We started the investigation on the second floor, in the room that had been Randy's bedroom. One investigator was using her dowsing rods. As with all interactive devices, we set protocol: cross the rods for yes, and open the rods for no (or leave them open for no if they were already open).

Dowsing rods have been used to detect underground water, metal, or underground wiring for ages by locating a strong energy field. The motion of dowsing rods has been attributed to the ideomotor response (a psychological phenomenon in which a person makes motions unconsciously). Basically the rods move due to an involuntary movement by the person holding them.

To test this theory, a friend of mine had provided me

with a block of wood with two round holes to fit the handles of my mini dowsing rods. I was preparing to conduct an experiment to see if the rods would move without being held by a living person. One hole was slightly deeper than the other, so the rods would be able to cross, if applicable.

After setting protocol and spending half an hour asking questions with a known yes answer in hope the rods would cross, I deemed the experiment unsuccessful. Dowsing rods do indeed rely on a person's central nervous system to move.

During my investigations I had in mind a purpose (or intent) to help, not harm. I wondered if true intention could guide our involuntary movement (e.g., "My intention is to find water" or "My intention is to ask you yes and no questions in the hope that you will answer"). Then I set protocol while a fellow investigator was holding the rods.

I had asked investigators to set intention before every investigation for over a year now, with good results. This night was no exception.

"If you are a male, cross the rods." (Rods crossed: yes.)

"Did you die in this room?" (Rods opened back up: no.)

"Did you build the room in the basement?" (Rods remained open: no.)

"Were you old when you died?" (Rods crossed: yes.)

One of the local investigators asked about a man who used to live in the bedroom on the first floor. "Do you remember Jeff, who used to stay here in the bedroom downstairs?" (Rods remained crossed: yes.)

"Did you like him?" (Rods opened: no.)

"Do you think he was a goofy guy who drank too much?" (Rods crossed: yes.)

The local investigator said that Jeff used to hear footsteps and voices upstairs while staying in that room.

"Is Randy Gebhart here?" (Rods opened: no.)

Just then the EMF meter spiked to a 2.5 reading for a second. The investigator using the rods grew tired, and we ended that session.

Downstairs in the living room, we placed two Mini Maglite flashlights on the mantel over the large stone fireplace. They were twisted to the almost on position, to make them easier to manipulate. I set the protocol to turn on the flashlight for a yes answer and turn it off (or leave it off) for a no. I then asked if they understood how to turn on a flashlight. (One turned on.) I requested for the flashlight to be turned off so we could begin asking questions. The flashlight flickered slightly and turned off.

I said, "If your name is Randy, turn on the flashlight." (Flashlight did not turn on.)

After no response to questions of whether we were talking to a man or a woman, I asked, "Are you a child?" (Flashlight turned on.)

"Are you over the age of ten?" (Flashlight turned off.)

Anji Erickson, a fellow investigator, had brought her son of approximately eleven years of age to this investigation. This interested the young boy. He said, "If you like jokes, turn on the light." (Flashlight turned on.)

I noted that only the red flashlight was being used, so

I said I would go pick up the other one. In the dark the flashlight that remained on was so bright as I approached the mantel, I could not see to pick up the other flashlight. I said, "Oh, the light is in my eyes. I can't see." At that exact moment, the flashlight turned off.

As I returned to the area in which the team was standing, the young boy with us said, "Now it's dark in here, and I can't see. Can you turn on the light, so I can see?" (Flashlight slowly flickered, then turned on bright.)

We thanked the child for communicating. I am always amazed when we get such good flashlight communication. It takes a lot of energy to manipulate such devices. Since flashlights are either on or off, it fascinates me to watch the light slowly ramp up, flickering, to turn on and slowly ramp down to turn off.

While I was still hoping to connect with Randy Gebhart, it was getting late, so Anji and I went down to the basement to do a quick investigation. When we did not get any real-time response, we gathered up our equipment that had been recording during the investigation.

Upon review of my digital recorder, I discovered many EVPs. Sometimes the order of EVPs can tell a story. It is like putting a puzzle together, which can be difficult when you can't understand all the words being said.

Once the investigators left the basement after setting up the equipment, I could hear what sounded like a latch or a lock being opened. This was odd, because all the hanging hardware from the doors to the concealed area and the secret room had been removed. There was a male EVP that said, "Go to your mom," and the same noise of a latch or lock being moved.

"Come on, step on it . . . you want something?"

"Mom . . . Mom."

"What? Come on."

There was a series of unidentifiable words. Then there was the sound of a light switch being flipped and what sounded like an empty gun click, which repeated shortly after.

A few other words were captured, many of which I couldn't identify. Some sounded like "psst," as well as a "now" or "wow." Near the end, when I had gone downstairs with Anji, one of us asked, "Are you getting used to us being down here with you?"

The EVP response: "Go home."

"Tell me your parents' names."

"No."

"You can talk to us."

"No."

The furnace kicked back on, and we packed up and called it a night.

As I drove home, I thought about Randy's situation. He was charged with a crime, and I imagine he reasoned that death was the only way to avoid the distress of lawful procedure and consequences.

I didn't know Randy's life circumstances, but I did know that some people are at greater risk of committing a crime because of the conditions into which they are born. I thought about these possibilities.

I also thought about how most children are abused by someone they know and trust, which would have been the case with Randy's niece and her friends. What truly upset me was how close those three young girls were to possibly becoming victims.

I said a prayer for the safety and well-being of the girls and pondered the real reason that I was called to investigate the paranormal, which at this time was still unclear to me.

ELEVEN

The Opdyke House

By this time I was an accomplished investigator, utilizing a network of trusted paranormal colleagues. While continuing to research paranormal and supernatural phenomena, I found that there was a gap between science and spiritualism: people were mostly in one "box" or the other. Being so closed-minded with disbelief seemed to me just as unreasonable as believing too much. I feel it is important to have an open mind and develop your beliefs based on active investigation and consideration of what you discover.

My quest had been to document some of these divinations with digital camcorders and cameras in addition to the audio that I had successfully captured. One day I hoped to catch the holy grail of occurrences, whatever that may be.

I was preparing for an investigation that Steve Berryhill had arranged for us. The day before the investigation, I charged the batteries (and stockpiled extra batteries) for my camcorder and cameras. I put fresh batteries in my other devices and flashlights. We were going to investigate the Opdyke house, a historical home standing high on a hill overlooking Bellbrook.

Henry Opdyke, one of the founders of Bellbrook, built the Federal-style house between 1815 and 1825. According to George F. Robinson's *History of Greene County, Ohio*, Henry built the brick house on the farm and owned the land on which the west part of Bellbrook now stands.

Hailing from New Jersey, Henry moved to Ohio with his family, first settling in Montgomery County (at the corner of SR 725 and Wilmington Pike) before purchasing land in Bellbrook. He and his wife, Catherine, had nine children.

Henry came to an untimely death at the age of fifty-one while digging a well for a neighbor, after a mattock fell on him. Catherine lived another twenty-three years after Henry's death, passing away at the age of seventy-four.

Our investigation was set for the evening of June 29, 2012. During that afternoon a very destructive straight-line windstorm raced eastward across the Midwest at nearly 60 mph. This storm, termed "derecho," caused millions of dollars in property damage and massive power outages.

Members of our group began calling, inquiring if the investigation was still on. I replied with a resounding yes! How many times does an opportunity arise in which the whole town is without power? With no power and limited cell service, there would be the least electronic interference possible. We already had batteries charged and were ready to go.

Our group of all women arrived before dark. Before we finished setting up, I was walking through the house holding an EMF meter, when it suddenly spiked to 5.8! This was quite unusual, with no power sources working for miles, and it was an indication that this could be a very interesting night.

There were three sections to the Opdyke house. The first structure was a one-and-a-half-story brick house believed to have been built shortly after Henry purchased the land in 1815. A two-story brick addition was completed by 1825. Over fifty years ago, a more modern wooden addition was built on the west side.

Now 196 years old, the house was hidden by trees and overgrown brush. A developer owned the surrounding property, as well as the house, and had been building new luxury homes there for years.

The house was void of all furniture, and most of the building had been gutted, pending renovations, according to the developer. We chose the front parlor to start the investigation and placed folding chairs in there. I positioned my camcorder on a tripod in the back of the room, facing a fireplace wall that was decked out with built-in cabinets. Darkness had fallen, and the camcorder was running in infrared mode. Our human eyes can't pick up infrared light, but the sensors in digital camcorders and phones can . . . making the invisible visible.

The floor-to-ceiling fireplace surround and built-in mantel were made of oak and painted white. Two turned and fluted columns supported the raised breast, with a small mantel shelf on the bottom and a large, layered mantel shelf on the top. On each side of the fireplace were two sets of cabinets with doors, separated by two large drawers. The top cabinet held four shelves, and the bottom held two. The cabinets were also painted white. The large fireplace opening had been bricked closed and covered by sheetrock at some point, but the developers had smashed in part of the opening to see inside.

Time and the elements were taking their toll on the historic home. The house once owned by one of the founding fathers of Bellbrook was obviously being neglected by the developers who owned the property. Although we were told that the house was slated for renovation, why did they leave the doors and windows open for easy access to vandals and wild animals? We closed the doors the best we could, although much of the wood was warped from the effects of heat and dampness. We could close the windows just short of an inch or two, due to the distorted frames. Paint was peeling from the walls and built-ins. Most of the ceilings had been removed, exposing the rafters.

The simple staircase bore square spindles, with four decorative round balusters individually turned, each a little different from the others. A window on the landing between floors overlooked the west side of the knoll upon which the house sat. Despite the building's general run-down condition, the brick of the two-story house stood tall and stout, ready to withstand another couple decades. For now it appeared that the Opdyke house was well on its way to becoming a relic of time gone by.

Just before the start of the investigation, the camcorder picked up a white anomaly quickly moving from the middle of the fireplace into the rafters. It appeared to manifest near the small mantel shelf just above the fireplace opening, but when we reviewed the footage frame by frame, it seemed to come from the hole in the fireplace opening, gaining illumination as it rose to the height of the first mantel shelf and getting even brighter as it ascended to the rafters.

We positioned three Mini Maglite flashlights on the upper mantel shelf and placed two EMF meters side by side on the mantel. A K2 meter (another type of EMF device) was put on the lower mantel shelf. From this I learned that we offered too many choices of devices. Even so, spirit manipulating the devices seemed to choose one over another, only activating the devices of their choice. With no electricity for miles around, we sat in total darkness . . . until spirit began turning on the flashlights and/or manipulating the EMF devices to blink the red lights.

The adjoining room to the parlor on the north side was nailed shut. There were doors on the southwest side of the room that should have closed but wouldn't because of the swelled wood. They left a gap of about five inches.

About an hour into the investigation, we heard a noise in the adjoining room, as if a small rock had been thrown and hit the floor. A few seconds later, the camcorder caught an anomaly flitting from the direction of that room into the parlor. It fluttered above the flashlights and then jetted down. Just as the anomaly seemed to touch the center light, it instantly turned on! After that we began to get regular flashlight communication to our questions.

Using one of the EMF meters, we received no response when we asked if Henry Opdyke was with us; however, when we inquired if Catherine was there, the red lights blinked a yes, in accordance with the protocol that we had set earlier (blink once for yes and twice for no). The spirit that we knew as Catherine also favored the middle flashlight for answering questions.

After another hour of flashlight communication with who we believed to be Catherine Opdyke, we decided to go upstairs in the two rooms to conduct an EVP session. I brought the camcorder with us.

As it was a rather warm night, we only closed the downstairs windows. The upstairs windows were open, but screens were securely in place. We noticed that the two cedar closet doors were slightly open. We closed one door completely, in hope that we would get evidence of the door's opening, as it had seemed to open more (ever so slightly) upon our arrival upstairs. One of the ladies left her digital recorder running downstairs.

Spending more than an hour upstairs and with the windows open, we could hear a slight squeaking noise from time to time. It seemed to be coming from the parlor room downstairs. Frogs were singing their song outside that night, with the sound of someone's strumming an extended rubber band.

One of the ladies ventured downstairs alone to fetch a

new battery for my camcorder. As she ruffled through my camera bag looking for a battery in the dark, she felt as if she were being watched.

Half an hour later, we all returned to the parlor, hoping to communicate with Catherine once again. This time she was manipulating all three of the flashlights that we had left on the mantel. Previously favoring the flashlight in the middle, she was now lighting all of them up. It was like a "grand finale."

The time was nearing two o'clock when one of the ladies received a phone call from her husband that electricity had just been restored to their house. We decided to conduct one more EVP session before calling it a night. As we sat in the room during the darkest part of the night, we did not notice that the top of one of the parlor windows had been pulled down, opening the window from above, where there was no screen. Suddenly one of the ladies exclaimed, "Ooooh, what the hell?!"

Another said, "What?"

"A bat! Oh, shit!"

"Where? In here?"

"Yep! Right there!"

"Oh Jesus God!"

"No, it's not gone."

Nervous laughter. The same woman said, "'Oh, Jesus God,' not 'gone.'"

Just then the bat dive-bombed us.

Group scream: "Oh my God!"

"This is awful!"

Group laughter.

Holding my lantern on top of my head, I said, "How are we going to get our equipment out?"

The bat flew into the hallway by the front door, and one woman urged, "Close the door, close the door!" But the swollen wooden door would not close all the way. Relieved, I stood up to begin dismantling the equipment when suddenly the bat flew back into the room through the crack of the closed door.

We all screamed.

Someone yelled, "Open the door, open the door!"

One lady said, "Poor little thing."

Another yelled, "Poor little thing?"

Then a group scream arose, as the bat once again flew low across the room. "We're attracting them."

"Get away! Scat! Shoo!"

"Shut the door, shut the door!"

I turned my lamp on, and others turned on their flashlights. We were finally able to gather our equipment, fold up our chairs, and call it a night—a successful paranormal investigation.

As I drove home, it dawned on me that we had closed the windows as much as we could, leaving just one or two inches open at the bottom, where the screens were. It was now obvious that the bat had flown through the window in the parlor room. I was beginning to smell a rat. I wasn't about to go back alone now, at almost three o'clock in the morning, but I did go back the next day.

~

Sure enough, the next day upon my return, one of the parlor room windows that we had closed was wide open from the top down. This explained the "squeaks" we'd heard while investigating upstairs.

I gathered everyone's digital recorders and personally reviewed them. The recorder left running in the parlor while our group of ladies was upstairs told the tale. As I expected, our investigation had been compromised. The audio recording confirmed that two intruders had walked into the parlor while we were upstairs investigating. I could clearly hear two sets of heavy footsteps and a manly cough, as one slowly pulled the top of the parlor window down, causing the occasional squeaks. I was disappointed to hear this contaminating evidence and frightened by the idea that one of the women could have been in danger, as she went downstairs alone to bring up a newly charged battery . . . until I heard a female EVP. As the footsteps were revealed and the window squeak was heard, a gentle female voice said, "Cowards!" I believe Catherine Opdyke had no respect for those two men who had happened upon our investigation.

A final review revealed that we had captured another video of a light anomaly in the parlor and captured an EVP that said, "Hey," and another that said, "Hide." I heard a couple taps on one of the recorders, but that had to be disregarded because of the intruders. The most impressive experience that night was the extreme flashlight action.

This was the first investigation in which I experienced multiple flashlights being used as communication tools, and seeing all of them turn on at the same time, I was amazed.

⁓

A few years later, it was obvious that the developers had no intention of renovating the Opdyke house. They let it continue to fall into a state of disrepair. On July 18, 2016, the zoning officer for the city of Bellbrook issued a Certificate of Appropriateness, as requested from the developer. With this certificate the developer was able to procure a permit for residential demolition from Greene County on August 5. The Opdyke house would soon be no more. High on the hill, overlooking the city of Bellbrook, if renovated properly the Opdyke house could have provided a glimpse back in time. It could have been an iconic window into Bellbrook's Old Village area. After a fast and unsuccessful attempt by community members to save the property, the Opdyke house was destroyed on November 1. What was even more gut wrenching was the fact that the house of one of Bellbrook's founding fathers was demolished during the year of Bellbrook's bicentennial celebration. The remains of the notable house now rest at the Xenia Demolition Debris Facility: a dump.

The evening before the demolition, a friend and I went to the Opdyke house to say goodbye. My friend had helped fight a grand but ultimately unsuccessful battle to save the home. We stood inside the house, in the opening where the front door used to be, looking out over the hill and pasture that would soon become roads and expensive homes. We touched the bricks and symbolically offered the house to God, asking for peace and protection to those who may still dwell within; however, I could feel that the ghosts were gone.

TWELVE

House of Mirrors

The iron gate, standing six feet high and made of black rods, looked like it had been forged a century ago, but it was actually made to look that way. The motorized swing gates were open, since we were expected. The winding drive, flanked by rows of trees whose leaves had begun to drop due to the extreme heat of late summer, led to the distinct symmetrical sprawling mansion of a house.

As we rounded the final curve, we first saw the two-story log cabin that had been transported from another state and attached to the far end of the house. The cabin, made of handcrafted squared logs interfaced with dovetail corners, donned an added porch with four pillars and two porch swings. The dark red Colonial paned and paneled door seemed familiar and welcoming. The windows were small, like something you would see in old country cottages; the paintwork on the trim was brilliant white, making it exude old-world charm.

The first floor of all sections of the main house was clad

in natural quarry stone embedded with hues of an earthen sunrise. The second floor was encased with matching wood siding. As we drove onto the immense decorative stamped concrete parking area, the French Country architecture of the main entrance gave an inviting first impression.

An open gabled roof shielded the massive arched double wooden doors, inset slightly under a stone archway. The stones in the arch were much larger than those on the surrounding wall, with the keystone the biggest of all. The large old-style doors topped ten feet and were a brighter shade of red than the door to the log cabin. Two curved windows perfectly matched the arched panels and vintage doorknobs, and a round iron knocker struck a balance between rustic and elegant. Each side of the doors was adorned with a tall spiral evergreen topiary and a large antique cast iron lion statue, both sitting tall, symbolizing honor, respect, and power.

Coincidence had nothing to do with the fact that I would visit that same house twice this day. We had an investigation planned for the evening, but a daytime walk-through was scheduled to familiarize ourselves with the clients' home.

Two other investigators and I marveled at the allover beauty of the property, which sported a large pond, complete with a deck that jetted out almost to the middle by the large fountain, and a guest cottage that doubled as an art studio.

We stood before the large red doors in silent admiration. With no doorbell in sight, we used the ornate knocker to announce our arrival.

The door quickly opened, and there stood a lovely woman with blond hair and fair skin; red lipstick made her big smile glisten. "Hello!" said Lisa, as she motioned for us to enter. Lisa was a client before she became an investigator herself.

"Honey, the ghost hunters are here," she said, as her husband joined us in the foyer. After everyone exchanged pleasantries, we began hearing about the history of the house, its custom build with reclaimed materials, and the plethora of antiques throughout.

The foyer—which led to a hall providing access to the kitchen, dining room, billiards room, and stairs to the second floor—bore a raised gable-style ceiling joined with a dozen solid wood beams on each side that connected in a point at the top. These beams, along with decorated stenciled ones mounted on the adjoining living room ceiling, were repurposed from a Catholic church that had been demolished some time ago. The stone surround and hearth on the fireplace in that room were reclaimed from an old courthouse. A conservatory (a room with a glass roof and walls) was attached to the opposite end of the living room, and a large waterfall cascaded down the nearby hillside.

The dining room was furnished with a massive mirrored tabletop, a fabric-draped ceiling, and an old-world Tuscan-style black chandelier. The billiards room, decorated with massive wood window trim boasting family crest–shaped shields, resembled a fortified structure from the Middle Ages. The cushion bumpers and bed cloth of the billiards table were a muted red, almost the color of dried blood. Off the main hallway, there was an entrance to the library, where we could access the lower level of the attached log cabin. The wooden door from the library to the cabin was almost always left open. The lower level of the cabin was one large room, with an enormous fireplace at the far end. An early American wood burning fireplace—the kind that a pioneer family would have used—was sheathed in brick, with a twenty-six-inch fireplace crane rod used to hang a kettle for cooking. The majestic wooden mantel and apron were stained a dark brown, with a rectangular window design and matching pilasters. The area was set up as a family room, with a large leather couch, an overstuffed chair, an old church pew, and miscellaneous decorative items completing the comfy appearance. To the left of the fireplace was a floor-to-ceiling array of built-in cabinets and drawers of various sizes and colors, giving the space an *Alice in Wonderland* kind of look. To the right was a wall of solid white woodwork with a slim, and almost secret, door that led to a speakeasy beneath the room. Far to the right of the fireplace was an almost hidden staircase that led exclusively to the upstairs bedroom of the log cabin, formerly the master suite.

So far every room (with the exception of the kitchen and conservatory) had a large fireplace, which was the focal point of each space.

Newly completed renovations created a modern master bedroom suite on the second floor on the opposite side of the house. At the end of the old hallway, before entering the new master bedroom suite, was a treasured small stained-glass window held closed with an old-fashioned sliding latch. The stained glass design depicted a tree with a bird's nest in which two eggs were nestled. Lisa felt that this represented her two children, both now grown.

The entrance to the master suite was adorned on both sides with built-in closets enclosed by four French doors, each having fifteen mirrored panes. In a nook to the left, before entering the actual bedroom area, two white antique dressers with hutches held clothing essentials. The bed was positioned between two windows, with a cathedral ceiling above. Lisa had decorated the wall with large angel wings but was toying with the idea of replacing them with decorative silver plates. On the other side of the room was another nook, with French doors that led to a Juliet balcony and a smaller dresser totally encased in mirrors, in which she displayed some knickknacks and an antique mirror on top. The entrance to the white marble bathroom was through that nook. Another fireplace stood on the wall between the bathroom and bedroom entrance, with a flat screen television above the mantel.

As we toured the house, one of the investigators carried the owners' small dog, who never barked while being held.

After returning downstairs, we took a seat in the living room. Lisa offered us some refreshments. Then came the stories of the ghostly events that the homeowners had encountered.

In the living room, just around the corner from the foyer, five built-in shelves held dozens of small, framed family photos. Only one photo, on one of the higher shelves, was found regularly on the floor: the photo of

Lisa's departed mother. She had no idea why this occurred and consistently returned the photo to the shelf, only to find it back on the floor a few days later.

A step up from the living room revealed the custom eat-in kitchen, where a rustic, sunbaked round table welcomed guests. The wooden cabinets were fitted with soft close hinges and door slides, yet at times the sound of cabinet doors slamming shut could be heard throughout the lower level.

The dining room had an atmosphere of its own. The table and chairs, seating ten, created a coziness against the brown textured walls and white wainscoting extending around the room from the fireplace. What made this room unique was the abundance of mirrors. The large tabletop was mirrored, above the mantel the fireplace was mirrored, and an antique cabinet with a mirror stood tall in one corner. It is thought that mirrors can act as doorways for spirit activity. It should be noted that upon the first house renovation, the wiring had been replaced and upgraded to code; however, the homeowners experienced that the dining room lights flickered and sometimes would not work at all.

Several years earlier on Christmas Day, the family and their guests were sitting down to Christmas dinner, when the lights flickered. Lisa's teenage son yelled out, "Stop it, you stupid ghosts!" and instantly the lights turned off. Flipping the light switch provided no results. Sitting in darkness, Lisa said in a raised voice, "Don't listen to him. He's just a dumb kid," and the lights immediately turned back on.

There was also a habitual occurrence in the library: a small stack of books on the bottom shelf of a built-in to the right of the fireplace would be found moved and stacked on the floor.

The family said that the lower level of the attached log cabin seemed to expel negative energy, giving them an odd feeling upon entry.

Lisa noted a half cement wall in the room to the left of the bottom of the basement stairs, where they stored wine and liquor for parties. She explained that she and the woman who helped her clean watched a magnum of wine being moved to the edge of the wall, where it was then pushed off, broke, and splattered everywhere. It happened so quickly that neither could try to grab the large bottle. I opened the door to the basement and noticed a large mirror leaning against the wall across from the staircase. "Another mirror?" I thought to myself. Every room in this house had one (or more) possible windows into another world.

On the second floor of the log cabin, the closet door was found open on a regular basis. The door latched snugly when closed, and the homeowners could find no explanation for this. Footsteps were heard at random times from the upstairs hall, as well as on the lower level of the cabin.

On the other side of the second floor, Lisa opened the small stained-glass window next to their bedroom door. A robin's nest sheltering three eggs sat on the outside sill. The stained glass depicted a robin's nest with two eggs, representing her two children. Lisa was a bit overwhelmed to find this symbolic gift. When she delivered her second child, a small mass was discovered, indicating that she was originally pregnant with twins, and since she had been pregnant twice, this made for a total of three children. When she was sure that the nest had been abandoned, she brought it inside and put it in a place of admiration.

The homeowners had recently torn out two upstairs bedrooms to create the new master suite. During this time the construction crew reported unexplained experiences to their supervisor, who approached Lisa and asked, "Does your house happen to be haunted?"

She responded, "You bet!"

My friends and I returned for the investigation that evening, before darkness began to fall. Photos were taken outside just ahead of twilight; more were taken on the inside before lights were dimmed. With the property's size, taking what we call "control photos" took almost an hour. Those interested gathered and said a prayer of protection, asking God that even when afraid, we may put our trust in him. For me this is a regular routine before every investigation.

I set up an infrared camcorder at the end of the upstairs hallway, pointing toward the new master bedroom door. Digital recorders were placed in the living room and the first floor of the cabin. DVR cameras were set up in the library and dining room. Static devices were set up in two rooms upstairs, along with thermometers, to detect temperature changes. Two people carried and monitored different types of EMF meters, while others held their own digital recorders throughout the evening. My P-SB7 ghost box was in my back pocket, and I carried a handheld full spectrum (FS) video camera. At this point in my experience of paranormal investigating, all of this gadgetry was to help me gather potential evidence in a more scientific manner, with the ultimate goal of "proving" there was an afterlife . . . although this night I would have a personal experience that no scientific method could document.

Splitting into two groups, the homeowners, another investigator, and I began our investigation on the second floor. When I checked the infrared camcorder in the hall, it briefly went out of focus three times, although nothing appeared to block the lens. As I was making sure the settings were correct on the camera, out of the corner of my eye I saw Lisa's husband walk into the master bedroom and cross the room, casting a shadow across the opening of the door. I stood in the hall, waiting for him to come out of the bedroom, when he happened upon me from the other direction.

"Were you just in your bedroom?" I asked.

"No, I was in the cabin," he said.

"Is there another way out of the master bedroom suite?"

"No, just the door at the end of the hallway," he answered.

"I thought I saw you enter your room. I saw somebody go in."

While Lisa and the other investigator were sitting in the cabin, her husband and I walked into the master suite to find nobody there. We joined the other two in the cabin, and I fired up the ghost box.

"Is there anybody with us in this room?" I asked.

A male voice came through the ghost box and said, "Yes."

"I'm shitting my pants!" said Lisa.

We continued the ghost box session for about ten minutes. It can be difficult to decipher words coming through the box. That is why I record these sessions on a digital recorder; I can better understand what is being said during review, using headphones after the investigation.

After spending almost two hours upstairs, the groups rotated, one homeowner with each. As we walked toward the dining room, suddenly we heard what sounded like a kitchen cabinet open and close with a slam. "Holy shitballs! Did you hear that?" Lisa exclaimed. "Did you hear it?"

"Yes, I heard it," I said, as I went into the kitchen to find the cabinets all closed tightly. I rewound the digital recorder that was sitting in the living room, and sure enough, it had captured the unexplainable phenomenon.

As the others went into the library, I decided to pause the DVR camera in the library and observe the DVR monitor to see what was going on in the extremely mirrored dining room. There was quite a bit of orb-like activity. With a fabric-draped ceiling, it would have been no surprise that dust could have been floating around the room, reflecting as an orb in infrared camera mode. Suddenly I saw a bright white anomaly fly in from the right side of the monitor, stop and hover for a few seconds, and then return in the direction from which it had come.

I joined the others in the library. Since they were in the midst of using an EMF meter, engaging in conversation via yes and no questions, I headed to the entrance of the lower level of the cabin. As I stepped inside, my chest tightened and my breathing became a bit labored. I was overcome with an unwelcome feeling, yet I continued in, sitting on the couch. I sat quietly, looking around the room, using the moon's glow as a nightlight. Suddenly I heard a loud rumbling noise that startled me, and then I realized it was the others coming down the steps from the second floor.

It was midnight, and the other investigators were packing up to leave. They stated that when they began their investigation, the closet door was closed tightly in the cabin bedroom. Later they noticed that it was open about twelve inches; nobody knew when it had occurred. Since we did not have a camcorder stationed in that room, it would remain a mystery.

The investigation team was down to me and another woman. I was intrigued by the closet door's opening, just as Lisa had experienced on many occasions. The four of us went back upstairs to the cabin bedroom. I was running my FS handheld camcorder, as everyone took a seat. With no other chairs available, I sat on the corner of the bed, with my back to the closet door. We were chatting among ourselves, talking about how hot it was, when I heard Lisa speak up. In a frightened and shaky voice, she said, "Mar-ciaaaaaa . . . there is a shadow behind you!"

"Where?" I asked. "By the closet?"

"Yes. It is tall and thin. Now it is more toward the bed," said Lisa.

Before I could react, I felt an ice cold chill press against my entire back, and within seconds my teeth began to chatter.

With the camcorder running, I quickly stood, took a few steps away, and turned around. As I was looking for the shadow in the viewfinder of my camcorder, I panned by the closet door, which was closed. I panned to the side of the bed, and as I moved the camera back toward the closet, I saw that the door was now open. Lisa—in her "holy shitballs" mode—asked me to get out the "do-whopper-whopper," her term for the EMF meter that lights up. We walked to the adjoining room to retrieve it. Upon our return the closet door was closed, but not latched. Lisa's husband closed it and pulled on the knob to be sure that it would not simply pop back open (which it did not).

As he walked away, Lisa exclaimed, "Oh my God! It is in that corner, between the plates on the wall and the closet door! And your do-whopper thingy is going off!" When I moved the camcorder to that area, nothing showed up in the viewfinder.

We went into the adjoining room and turned on the ghost box; however, the ghost box was not working properly now. The scans were too fast, and the volume level had dropped. We decided to abandon the ghost box session.

As we walked back into the bedroom area, there it was in my viewfinder: a tall shadow, between six and seven feet tall, to the left of the closet door. I asked everyone to move to my left, to be sure I was not picking up any of our shadows. As they did, Lisa's wavering voice said, "You're not; he's there." The other investigator with me confirmed that she was seeing the same thing I was. To be sure, I asked everyone to kneel down, but the shadow remained. "What's your ghostbuster tool say?" asked Lisa.

"It just reads the EMF field, and right now I'm not moving from this spot," I said.

Just moments later, Lisa's husband walked over to the area, and the shadow disappeared. He saw nothing and felt nothing.

Lisa originally saw the shadow with her own eyes, but the rest of us could only see it through the viewfinder of the digital camcorder. The time now was one o'clock, and we decided to end the investigation. Lisa turned on the lights and ran to the restroom to avoid peeing her pants after that experience. Her husband told us that the room we were in was now the guest room and asked, since it was so late, if we wanted to spend the night. My fellow investigator gave me a quick glance and blurted out, "Hell, no! Your house is haunted!"

We packed up all the equipment, and I quietly said a closing prayer, gave our thanks, and said goodbye. I explained to the homeowners that I would begin uploading the files the next day and immediately begin the review process. With multiple recording devices placed all around the house, the review would be a massive undertaking, but I was up to the challenge.

⟶

Never in my life have I done such extensive work on technical evidence review. There was so much going on, it was like stepping into another universe. I forced myself to close the work on this investigation after a month of review.

I used Final Cut Express[1] editing software at this time, and I racked and stacked audio and video clips like a central data center. I handwrote the time code in a notebook, as I logged and transferred clips into the queue. I typed up a log of the most interesting clips, which turned out to be over twenty pages long. I burned the most pertinent clips to DVD, stored the original files on an external hard drive, and created a PowerPoint presentation for the homeowners and their family.

I began with the digital recorder left stationary in the dining room during the morning walkthrough of the house. I was happy when digital recorders became readily available, compared to the earlier mini cassette recorders that I had used as a newspaper reporter. Those cassette recorders could create their own noise with their moving parts. A digital recorder is a device that records sound and captures it as a file format that can be uploaded to a computer or tablet. When an EVP is captured, it is usually single words or short phrases. I only use what is termed Class A EVP, words captured that need no editing or filters to understand. This way I can't be accused of using sound processing techniques to find samples of audio buried deep within noise that I deem to be "a voice." It either is or it isn't.

The digital recorders and recorded ghost box sessions revealed that there were people living their lives around ours. We could not see each other, but we certainly could hear them. It reminded me of a quote from Anthony Horowitz, an English novelist: "There are two worlds. The world you understand and the world you don't. These worlds exist side by side, sometimes only centimeters apart, and the great majority of people spend their entire lives in one without being aware of the other. It's like living in one side of a mirror: you think there is nothing on the other side until one day a switch is thrown and suddenly the mirror is transparent. You see the other side."[2]

This house was nothing but one big mirror—actually a few hundred mirrors, many of them antique. Antique mirrors usually have a silver metal coating on the back, and silver is a most notable metal. Silver has the highest electrical and thermal conductivity of all metals and one of the greatest optical reflectivities. Silver does not react with other substances. Silver atoms and their electrons are not densely packed. Electrons (that carry electricity) interact with visible light waves, which cause the electrons at the surface of the silver to move, causing the light to reflect back. Now here is where it gets interesting. When infra-red light frequencies (lower light frequencies) are used with a silver-backed mirror, electrons can match the speed of the slower infrared frequencies and reflect them back;

however, with some higher light frequencies, such as ultra-violet light, the electrons can pass right through the mirror. (Glass is a material that does not distort such a light wave but absorbs it, allowing it to pass through.) If spirits do indeed have an electromagnetic field in the higher light range of frequency, the silver back on the mirror may be attractive as a doorway for possible spirit movement.[3]

The daytime walkthrough revealed a conversation among a man, a woman, a young boy, and his dog. While the homeowners' small dog was held throughout the tour without barking, I heard a dog barking constantly on the recorder. A male voice said to the barking dog, "Fetch your bone."

"You haven't been good," he said.

"You're in trouble," the female voice added.

Male voice: "Don't do that."

A different male voice: "Go back."

Another male voice: "Get him?"

Original male voice: "Romeo, come here."

During review of the outside control photos, we found what appeared to be a young boy looking down from an upstairs window, with his dog beside him. The dog appeared to have one black ear and one white ear, totally unlike the homeowners' dog.

Recordings from both the walkthrough and the investigation gave us snippets of conversation in between our talking and human noise contamination. Much of the digital conversation was inaudible due to these circumstances.

In another sitting I asked, "Were you killed in an accident?"

Other investigator: "Were you killed in a farming accident?"

Male voice: "Run over."

Me: "Were you sick?"

Male voice: "No."

Me: "Did you have any children?"

Male voice: "No. I never had that."

Female voice: "And you left me for that?"

Keep in mind that we could not hear the answers to our questions until we were reviewing the recordings afterward with headphones.

A few minutes later, I asked, "Do you want to tell us something?"

Male voice: "Said it."

Male voice: "Get out."

Me: "Do you need help?"

Male voice: "Nope."

While in the library, I requested that a light be manipulated on a device sitting on the table. When the light turned on, I said, "Thank you."

A female voice replied, "You're welcome."

From the recorder that sat in the darkness of the main room in the log cabin came words that explained the negative feeling I felt when I entered. We made suggestions of how to brighten that room and bring calmness to the space.

The evening I presented the reveal, Lisa prepared a

grand spread of food and invited family and friends. Not only was this the biggest investigation that I had ever been on, but it was also the largest crowd that had gathered to see the results. This was entertainment at its best for some of them, and all were hungry for excitement. The ghosts of Lisa's house did not disappoint. By the time I finished my reveal, her brother-in-law declared, "Don't think we are going to come over and water your plants when you're on vacation!"

Notes

1. Apple, Inc. discontinued the video editing software Final Cut Express in favor of Final Cut Pro X in June 2011. I continued to use Final Cut Express by not updating the operating system on my MacBook Pro.
2. Anthony Horowitz, *Raven's Gate*. Scholastic Press.
3. Richard Palmisano, *Are Mirrors a Portal for Ghosts?*

CHANCE ENCOUNTER

THIRTEEN

The Ghosts Walk with Jonathan Winters

"As summer fades and autumn's chill begins, there is another reason for shivers to run up and down your spine. The autumn months traditionally signal the approach of Halloween and trigger thoughts of ghosts and haunted houses. Come to Bellbrook, where you will walk the town after the sun goes down," reads my media release.

After two years of paranormal investigating, researching the folklore, and learning the history of Bellbrook, I decided it was time to have some fun by organizing a ghost walk and historical tour for interested community members.

There was much interest in the tour, as people were captivated by seeing what potential evidence I had captured over the past two years in their spirited little town, and the local folklore sparked their imagination. The Winters-Bellbrook Community Library opened for the first tour, serving as a refreshment area and displaying seasonal books. The building dates back to 1901 and has been offering library services to the community since 1906. The original building, a mere 595 square feet, was opened as a bank. When the bank failed, Jonathan Harshman Winters I[1] (president of Winters National Bank and the grandfather of comedian Jonathan H. Winters III) acquired the building. In 1906, he donated it to the Sugarcreek Township trustees, with a deed restriction requiring that the building be used only as a library.[2] In 1987, the deed was transferred to the city of Bellbrook. There have since been two additions—one in 1965 and another in 1980.[1]

Also still located in the Old Village area are the summerhouse and outbuildings of Clara Winters, the comedian's spinster aunt. While it was too far away to easily include in the ghost walk, I decided to present photographs of the home, the gatehouse, the carriage house, and a large chicken coop. The property has been updated and is currently being used as a residence.

A friend suggested that I have a "celebrity" connection to the ghost walk, and we put on our thinking caps. Bellbrook also has a claim to fame through American humorist Erma Bombeck, who, according to retired mayor Mary Graves, lived in Bellbrook. In one of her books, Erma wrote that she gave whiskey to ducks that she was keeping in her bathtub. Mary explained that this anecdote wasn't entirely true. "I just happened to stop by for a visit," she said, laughing. "She had ducklings in the bathroom, all right, but she did not put them in the tub or give them whiskey. She just let them have the run of the room, and when they were big enough, the children returned them to the pond." By the time of the first ghost walk, Erma had been dead for almost fifteen years. We decided to go the route of naming the first ghost walk after someone still living: hence, the Jonathan Winters Ghost Walk and Historical Tour of Bellbrook. I asked my friend how we would go about getting permission to use Jonathan Winters's name, and she said, as she walked away, "I'm sure you will think of something, Marcia!"

I began searching the internet. There were plenty of "hits" regarding Jonathan Winters's movies and TV shows; websites such as wikipedia.org had lots of statistics about him, but no contact information. I was about to give up when I came across a website selling Winters's rather strange art, CDs, and books—nothing more. The selection was limited, and I found an email address for a man named Joe. I emailed Joe something like this:

"Hello! I am organizing Bellbrook, Ohio's, first Ghost Walk and Historical Tour this year [2010]; and since the Winters family has a tie to Bellbrook and the Dayton area, if you happen to know Jonathan Winters (the comedian), would you mind asking him if we could name the event in his honor?" I left my cell phone number and hit "send," figuring that the email would hang out there in the internet's junkyard of unanswered messages forever.

Five days later I was meeting with the director of the Bellbrook-Sugarcreek Chamber of Commerce when my cell phone rang. At first glance I thought it was a school board member calling, and I excused myself to take the call. I answered the phone to find that it was Jonathan

Winters himself, calling from Montecito, California! I was so excited to get this unbelievable opportunity that I motioned to the director to give me a pen and some paper so I could take notes.

"Hi, this is Jonathan Winters—Jonathan without an 'H,'" he started out. He was "on," pretty much doing his act.

I broke into his conversation to get on record why he was calling. "Mr. Winters, do you mind if we name the ghost walk in your honor? The Jonathan Winters Ghost Walk and Historical Tour of Bellbrook?" I asked.

"Sure, oh sure. That's why I'm calling," he said. "Bellbrook is very small, almost a village, but very Americana. Just the sound of it: Bellbrook . . . American town . . . clean. I still remember the post office and the library."

He continued. "I worked at Wright Field and the big white box company. I had friends from Moraine city; they were rednecks from Kentucky. They worked at the big white box company too."

"The big white box company?" I asked.

"Yes, there were me and Merle. We worked in the box eight by ten feet high . . . ice cubes in the top and fake vegetables below . . . you know, the Frigidaire," he said.

"Oh! My grandfather worked for Frigidaire. I remember going to the company picnics when I was a little girl."

"Oh, you must be a wee little thing," Jonathan said, laughing. "I still can't believe I worked with those clowns!"

He talked about his family: two children and five grandchildren. Only one grandchild was working, and that was at Starbucks. His grandchildren called him Bop-o.

"When I was younger, I went to a lot of movies. Frankenstein and Wolf Man all scared me to death," said Jonathan. "I'd like to go to New York for the premiere of the new Smurf movie; I am the voice of Papa Smurf. I was Grandpa Smurf in the first movie."

"I remember watching one of your first movies in the big theater at the Dayton Masonic Center near downtown Dayton: *It's a Mad, Mad, Mad, Mad World*," I said (a 1963 comedy about the madcap pursuit of $350,000 in cash stolen by a diverse group of strangers). That brought a resounding belly laugh from the comedian.

"I loved the Dayton Art Institute that's near the Masonic Center," he said. "I used to stay in a house next door to it that housed artists. It's gone now."

I later learned that Jonathan was a master painter. He attended Kenyon College, hoping to pursue a career in fine arts. He later enrolled at Dayton Art Institute. He studied cartooning in Dayton, where he met his wife, Eileen.

Jonathan went on to say that he had lost his wife in 2009. He said that his health wasn't great, having had three stints and four pacemakers, but he was glad to be a Buckeye.

I replied, "Yeah, me too, although a buckeye is just a worthless nut!"

The comedian of sixty years broke out in laughter. He laughed as if he had never laughed before. After a minute he calmed down and said, "I'm going to use that line!"

I then asked him about his aunt Clara's summerhouse and whether he had any memories of it. He was surprised and asked if it was still standing. I told him that it sure was, complete with the outbuildings. Another chuckle arose when he told me how his mother would take him to visit his spinster aunt in the summer. "I remember, as a kid around seven or eight years old, visiting my aunt. I recall this huge brass box on the table that always had orange sponge cake in it. She would tell me to help myself. Hmm . . . saying that to a husky boy like me, well, I ate the whole thing!" said Jonathan. "She'd get after me. I remember her bent over, using a cane to help her walk. She never married and was quite a character."

"By any chance, did you create the character of Maude Frickert after your aunt Clara?" I inquired.

Laughing, he said, "Oh, Maudie . . . she sure was like my aunt Clara!"

I asked if he would like me to send photos of Aunt Clara's house, and he graciously accepted. "You know, one night I slept in the gatehouse," he said. "It was too hot in the main house." The wooden frame that used to hold a small mattress still existed in the gatehouse in 2010. After Jonathan gave me his mailing address, he said, "Hey, how about those Reds? They are doing well this year," and that was the end of our conversation.

Not too long after, I mailed Jonathan Winters photographs of the inside and outside of his aunt Clara's house, along with a letter telling him how we collected buckeyes every autumn from two very large and mature trees on the bike trail in Greene County. They were usually quite large, and I referred to them as "gourmet buckeyes." Approximately three weeks later, I received another phone call from Jonathan, thanking me for the photographs and asking if I would send him some of those "gourmet buckeyes" in the fall. "You know I always carry a buckeye in my pants pocket," he said. I did not know that, and I assured him that I would be happy to send him some buckeyes when they fell from the trees. He sounded a bit down, explaining that he had fallen and broken his collarbone. He wasn't feeling well and had to go.

That September, a month before the first ghost walk in his honor, I collected the buckeyes, as I had promised. Not knowing how many he wanted, I decided to send him a small box with about thirty of them. He mentioned that he liked to give one away on occasion to friends.

It wasn't long after that I received yet another phone call from Jonathan Winters. Upon answering the phone, I said, "Hello."

Jonathan proceeded to bellow, "Enough already!" as he laughed. "I only wanted a couple of buckeyes! When I opened the box, there were so many, they rolled everywhere, even falling on the floor!"

I jokingly apologized. I could tell he still wasn't feeling like his old self.

During an earlier call, I had encouraged him to crash Kim Kardashian's wedding to Kris Humphries, as it was to be held in the city in which he lived. I took the opportunity now to ask him if he had indeed attended the Kardashian wedding on August 20. He mustered a laugh and assured me that he had not.

That was the last time I spoke with Jonathan Winters.

On October 2, 2010, the first Jonathan Winters Ghost Walk and Historical Tour was held in the city's chambers. We had a good turnout, and the presentation seemed to amaze most of the attendees; however, while the presentation began with a brief history of comedian Jonathan Winters and his connection to Bellbrook, I was surprised to discover that most of the younger folks in attendance had no idea who he was. The first ghost walk took place forty-nine years after Jonathan's first movie was released (when I was eight years of age). When I realized this, boy, did I feel old!

The next year I reluctantly excluded Jonathan Winters's name from the title of the ghost walk, and in 2013, the year he died, I held the ghost walk in his memory. Later in 2013, the Office of the Mayor of Bellbrook, Ohio, issued a proclamation recognizing the outstanding significance of comedian Jonathan Winters's ties with Bellbrook.[3]

My friend Steve Berryhill, a lifelong community resident, has cornered the market on conducting historical tours of the Old Village of Bellbrook and its cemetery. He has been involved with the Bellbrook-Sugarcreek Historical Society[4] longer than I can remember. For many years he guided the school's annual third-grade tour. Those students would walk in groups from Bell Creek Intermediate to learn fun facts, such as who founded their town and how Bellbrook got its name.

When I decided to organize a ghost walk, Steve gave me a personal tour to help me learn more about the historical homes and buildings. All I had to do was add the ghosts!

Each year the group of people assisting me with the ghost walks varied. My first goal was to find knowledgeable people to be tour guides so we could walk three groups at a time. I enjoyed being a tour guide, but with the tricky setup of my computer equipment and projector for the presentation before the walk, I usually had to stay behind during the tour to immediately pack up so the facility we were using could be locked.

What was unique to my ghost walks was that I always arranged to let the tour groups go inside what was believed to be a haunted location. Since private owners and organizations opened their doors during the tours, I needed to be available to stop in at all of these locations to be sure things were going according to plan and the participants were safe and being respectful of the properties. For this I needed additional volunteers. To protect the interests of the property owners, organizations, the city, myself, and the volunteers, participants were required to sign a waiver.

I was lucky to have several local people willing to help. Steve helped the first year, and Barry Tiffany, the administrator and director of development for Sugarcreek Township, participated in the ghost walks for years.

Since so many of us had been involved in the paranormal investigation of most of the buildings on the tour, I thought it would be interesting for the investigators to give the tour groups some insight on their experiences inside the buildings that we could not take them into.

Barry moved to the Bellbrook area when he was in the fourth grade (so he just missed out on Steve Berryhill's third-grade tour) and graduated from Bellbrook High School in 1978. This made him a perfect tour guide and watchman for the privately owned properties open for the ghost walks. He also had a strong interest in the paranormal, once conducting a psychometry demonstration (the ability to discover facts about a person by touching inanimate objects associated with them) and pointing out areas of interest in some of the haunted buildings.

In the following years, I really didn't need to advertise the ghost walk and historical tour, as Barry had recruited a large group of friends and relatives to attend.

At the first ghost walk, I established an age restriction of twelve and older. While many ghost walks and haunted attractions during the season of Halloween are usually considered entertainment with a "fun" scare, I felt that having actual buildings in which I'd had several ghostly experiences open to participants wasn't appropriate for younger children.

However, some of my grandchildren attended investigations with me from time to time. My then twelve-year-old granddaughter and her friend assisted me with setting up chairs and tables for the second presentation, and both looked forward to going on the ghost walk with my group. While the girls had a blast, the screams and giggles along the way as we walked through the residential neighbor-hood at night helped me make the decision to limit future events to a minimum of sixteen years of age.

As the three tour groups took their turns inside the now deemed "haunted house," Dave Jones and Barry were manning the upstairs, showing the attendees how to con-duct EVP sessions and properly use a digital camera during an investigation. While there were no zombies or killer clowns involved in my event, there were definitely some ghostly encounters.

Dave was using his digital recorder, hoping to capture ghostly voices during the tours; however, he would need to stop, rewind, listen, and analyze the data during the event to share any potential evidence. To provide more of an "instant gratification" for attendees, he turned on his P-SB7 spirit box, which he mounted on a stand and connected to an external speaker. The P-SB7 spirit box, or "ghost box," as we call it, is a voice generator and should not be mistaken as a device to record EVPs. And voices and words were heard that night, to everyone's amazement. Responses are gener-ally brief, and the attendees were thrilled when they finally heard a recognizable word: "Hello." Some were astounded, while others felt it was just the fallibility of human percep-tion.

When I held the ghost walk the following year, that same building gave our tour groups some interesting expe-riences. Barry's guests, my volunteers, and I stayed after the event ended to conduct an extended investigation together. Barry's sister, Brenda, seemed to connect with someone who she felt was a female child. We had situated a Mini Maglite flashlight on the mantel above the fireplace, turning it just far enough to stay in the off position. Brenda engaged the child in a game of hide-and-seek, using the flashlight.

"Turn on the flashlight, and I'll go hide," said Brenda. When the flashlight turned on, Brenda would slowly walk backward into the small hallway and hide behind the wall, approximately three feet deep. The flashlight would turn off as she was hiding.

"If you want me to come out, turn the flashlight back on," Brenda said. The flashlight would turn back on, and Brenda would slowly come out, walking and talking as if playing with a small child.

This scenario went on for almost twenty minutes. I was growing weary of the same game over and over, but I let it continue since we were hosting the event. Once again Brenda began backing up into the corner of the hallway to hide. Just as she disappeared behind the wall, we all heard a loud growl! Brenda did not seem frightened. She started her childlike walking in the other direction, back into the living room, saying, "Guess I'm not going to hide again!"

I recalled that a man named Eugene Belden had lived a long time in that house. He was a city councilman for eight years. Records show that he had worked at NCR and was missing three fingers on one hand. Shortly after purchasing the house, the current owner's son was mowing the grass. He felt as if he was being watched. He stopped mowing, looked up, and in the window of the small rear bedroom on the second floor, saw a man looking at him. It was a quick glimpse; the boy's description was an older man with a drawn face, almost skeletal. Upon second glance, the figure was gone. I wondered if Eugene's spirit had become fed up with the constant game of hide-and-seek and let his impatience be known by giving us the human snarl that we all heard.

After that a couple of our guests decided to leave, but the rest of us remained. I set up a mini DVR and put a wireless camera in the butler's pantry. A flashlight was also placed on a shelf there. Brenda went into the room to ask questions, hoping that the flashlight would turn on in response. Barry shared with me that Brenda had lost her son in an accident a couple years prior. That horrific experience sparked her interest in the paranormal. Little did I know at that time that I too would soon be coping with the extreme sadness of the loss of a child.

The butler's pantry was small. I manned the DVR monitor, while Brenda tried to establish flashlight communication with a spirit by asking yes and no questions (turn the flashlight on for a yes answer and leave it off or turn it off for a no). The camera was automatically in infrared mode, as it was dark outside and we had the lights turned off. I don't recall the questions that Brenda was asking as she was getting the flashlight to turn on and off. What I found incredible that night, as I watched Brenda in the monitor, was seeing a small, bright anomaly slowly travel from the far wall across the butler's pantry, continue its path right in front of Brenda, and then turn to its right to exit the room and move down the hall. As it turned from Brenda, a trail of twinkling essence could be seen as it passed by the camera. Barry was looking over my shoulder and said, "I hope that camera is recording." It most certainly was!

We decided to do a session upstairs in one of the bedrooms. There was limited furniture throughout the house. In this particular room were a desk, two chairs, and a small table. We laid three Mini Maglite flashlights on the table. Barry had several people in the room with him, including two of my best friends. As he was asking questions, neither of the flashlights turned on, but two of them began to move. The flashlight on the end, to the left of the onlookers, rolled slightly toward the edge, stopping just short of rolling off the table. The flashlight in the middle was slowly rocking back and forth. When it stopped, it had not moved any further than the spot from which it was initially laid down. The third flashlight never moved at all.

While this amazed some, it frightened others, including my two good friends. A few began working out scientific theories, and others were simply in awe of what they had just experienced.

All in all, that ended the investigation for the night. It was time to pack up, lock up, and call it another successful event.

Notes

1. Lisa P. Rickey, *Glancing Backwards*.
2. *Sesquicentennial Program and History of Bellbrook, Ohio*, June 1966.
3. City of Bellbrook website, http://www.cityofbellbrook.org
4. Bellbrook Historical Society, *Bellbrook 1816–1981*.

CURIOUS CONNECTIONS

FOURTEEN

Seven Sightings

Over the course of a decade's investigations in Bellbrook, there was one common thread: the regular sighting of a young girl scampering around the Old Village area.

The girl's approximate age was between six and eight years. She wore a cornflower-blue short-sleeved cotton prairie-style dress with a white apron, or pinafore. The hemline stopped short of the ankles, making it easy to see that she walked barefoot. Her long, blond hair had subtle waves, and she sported matching ribbons in her hair. She was always seen with a smile on her face.

The first sighting was at "the parsonage," where, during a paranormal investigation, the little girl let it be known that she used to live across the street and was killed in a fire. After some research, we found that indeed there was a fire on the night of April 30, 1919, during which eight buildings were destroyed, beginning on the northeast corner of Franklin and Main Streets. "Across the street" from the parsonage would put that area almost smack dab in the middle of the path of destruction; however, records do not show any deaths from it.

I believe the disembodied voice we heard at the parsonage was indeed she. It was the laughter of a young girl, and she seemed to be enjoying getting our attention. Several friends had a feeling that her name may have been Sarah.

She had been seen several times at Sugarcreek Elementary, the parsonage, and the museum—across different years, by different people. Most sightings were by friends of mine who also researched the paranormal; however, one sighting cemented the fact that this little girl roamed the Old Village.

My phone rang one morning around seven thirty. It was Sheila Woody, assistant to the superintendent of schools. At this time I was a former employee of the school district. Sheila was aware that I worked in the paranormal field, and her voice sounded rather excited as she quickly spoke. "Marcia, I had to call and tell you what I just experienced," she said.

"What was that?"

"I was leaving the grocery store in the early dawn hours, driving on the alley in the plaza, when suddenly I saw a little girl with blond hair run in front of me. She smiled as she ran across the lane. I put on the brakes, and she ran through the back wall of the Presbyterian church!"

I asked her what she was wearing. "A blue dress," Sheila said, "with a white apron."

I asked if she was wearing any shoes, and she replied, "No. She was barefoot."

I told her that she was the seventh person to report this sighting to me. Sheila had recently lost her husband to cancer . . . and little did I know I would soon lose my son. I believe this sighting brought her comfort, and it instilled in me that there is indeed life after death—all because of a little spirit girl running around wearing a blue dress and a smile of faith, love, and hope.

Sarah was a very common name in the 1900s. Acting on a hunch, I researched the local cemeteries in the Bellbrook area. My research included the Bellbrook Cemetery, the Pioneer Cemetery, the Fairview Primitive Baptist Church Cemetery, and the Middle Run Primitive Baptist Church Cemetery.

According to online documents posted on the City of Bellbrook website, there are eighty-four Sarahs buried in the area (various spellings of the name). None of them died in 1919, and none died between the ages of six and eight. There are no deaths listed on April 30, 1919. There is only one death listed in the month of May 1919, and that was for a seventy-seven-year-old man. I also walked the cemeteries. The older stones were almost impossible to read, so the spreadsheets on the city's website were very helpful. Running into dead ends on a hunch is common, and I take the time to do the research, so I am not guessing. It is quite possible that we have not seen the last of this mysterious little girl.

FIFTEEN

Orbs, Anomalies, and More

The definition of the word "orb" is "a spherical body or a globe." The definition of the word "anomaly" is "something that deviates from what is standard, normal or expected." The highly debated phenomenon of round balls of light that sometimes appear in photographs and video is usually shoved into the category of orbs. I believe observances of such things, whether in matter or spirit, should be classified as anomalies, because they definitely divert us from what we perceive normal to be, and we certainly don't expect them. For the sake of the majority of people who refer to all of these round globules as orbs, I will refer to them in this chapter accordingly, although I really mean anomaly.

These little balls of light that show up in photographs are usually dubbed by the skeptic as dust and by the believer as ghosts or spirits. (There is a difference between a ghost and a spirit.) Are they the consciousness of a soul? Is something else harnessing this energy, resulting in what we call orbs? Or is it dust?

Before I tackle the subject of orbs, let's talk about consciousness. While death is an inevitable consequence of life, studies have shown that awareness may continue even after the brain has shut down. Science and spirituality (which includes what I now call "transnormal" research) have been at a crossroads for some time. There have been many studies by doctors about near death experience (NDE) cases, in which patients were revived after being declared dead. These people had memories during the period that they were dead and were able to account for activities going on in the room at that time.

At the University of Virginia School of Medicine, there is a long-established research group exclusively devoted to the investigation of phenomena that challenge mainstream scientific paradigms regarding the nature of the mind-brain relationship. Founded in 1967, the Division of Perceptual Studies[1] (DOPS) researches phenomena related to consciousness clearly functioning beyond the confines of the physical body, as well as phenomena that are directly suggestive of postmortem survival of consciousness.

There are books written by scientists who themselves had unexpected conscious experiences they could not explain. One such book, *Infinite Awareness: The Awakening of a Scientific Mind,*[2] by Marjorie Hines Woollacott (foreword written by Pim van Lommel[3]), said, "She wanted to write this important, groundbreaking, and open-hearted book, which has the potential to change permanently our ideas about the interface between consciousness and the brain." The author, a neuroscientist, experienced a transcendent level of awareness during an attempt to try meditation to calm her fears about flying.

According to Marjorie, many scientists believe consciousness is only a product of a functioning brain; however, the books *Irreducible Mind*,[4] by Edward F. Kelly, Emily (Williams) Kelly, Adam Crabtree, Alan Gauld, Michael Grosso, and Bruce Greyson, and *Beyond Physicalism*,[5] edited by Edward F. Kelly, Adam Crabtree, and Paul Marshall, share documented research from key scholars in the areas of quantum physics, psychology, Asian philosophy, and mysticism to reconcile science and spirituality. These books are not easy reads. Edward said that *Irreducible Mind* is intended for the advanced undergraduate and early-stage students in subjects such as psychology, neuroscience, and philosophy.

Edward began his introduction in *Beyond Physicalism* with a quote from William James that reads: "Round about the accredited and orderly facts of every science there ever floats a sort of dust-cloud of exceptional observations, of occurrences minute and irregular than to attend to .... Any one will renovate his science who will steadily look after the irregular phenomena. And when the science is renewed, its new formulas often have more of the voice of the exceptions in them than of what were supposed to be the rules."[6]

This is where I feel orbs and anomalies are classified—not that orbs float in "a sort of dust-cloud" (no pun intended), but in the exceptional observations of occurrences.

I especially agree with the quote from Alfred N. White-head, an English mathematician and philosopher also mentioned in the introduction: "The rejection of any source of evidence is always treason to that ultimate rationalism which urges forward science and philosophy alike."[7]

This is why I encourage people to keep an open mind. Open-mindedness is one of the most important characteristics that we have. Being open-minded removes your personal biases and prejudices from all situations and lets you immerse yourself into another experience. It doesn't mean you have to agree; it simply means you are willing to consider someone else's perspective and then create your own conclusion.

The dust orb does exist. It is a common occurrence in photography. The bright white circles are usually caused by the flash of your camera illuminating particles of dust. Dust orbs are typically close to the camera lens and appear a bit blurry. They float in a haphazard fashion. There is no frame of reference for distance in a photograph of dust orbs, meaning there is no proof that the orbs are anywhere other than near the camera lens. These are reflections, not orbs.

Some will insist that everything round found in photographs is dust. We've all seen a beam of sunlight in which thousands of dust particles are floating in the air. Molecules colliding with dust particles and making them move causes this. So with thousands of dust particles moving around, how does the camera's flash sometimes only reflect "one" dust particle?

On several occasions I've captured orbs making intentional movements on video. One impressive example was when an orb moved into the frame from the right, stopped and hovered for a few seconds in the center of the frame, and then did a U-turn and exited in the direction from which it came. I highly doubt that this was a random act of molecules bumping into particles, to travel in such a deliberate manner.

In 2014, I captured what I truly believe to be a paranormal orb. I was with a group doing a daytime investigation at the Thompson House, an 1820s-era mansion located in Newport, Kentucky. In 1860, John T. Thompson, the inventor of the Tommy gun (Thompson submachine gun) was born there.[8] Today the house is a live music venue and art gallery.

My friend Jen and I had split off from the group and gone to the third floor, hoping to get into the highest room that led to the cupola; however, it was locked. As we stood on the stairs, we both heard a loud noise on the floor below, between a thump and a knock. It got our attention, and as Jen descended the stairs all the way down to the second floor, I stopped on the landing between floors and began taking photos. Because of the house's incarnation as a music venue with several small taverns, the décor was rather unique. The stairs from the second to third floor were painted red with purple walls. The hallway on the second floor was adorned with animal print carpet, with the other stairs from the second to first floor painted gold. The doors and wood trim were painted mustard yellow.

Reviewing my photos after the investigation, I discovered that I may have captured something remarkable, so I emailed them to my friend and fellow researcher Dave Margerum, who helped assess them.

In the first photo, an orb was captured in the open doorway furthest away from me. Since it was in the open door area, we had no reference of distance. Zooming in on the photo, Dave noticed that the orb had a mottled shading on its surface and a brighter edge on its peripheral. To the left of the orb, a single globe light fixture hung just below the ceiling beam, with a white piece of paper or label just above and slightly to the right of the light. There was nothing conclusive in the first photo to classify this as paranormal.

The next photo in the series showed that the orb had moved upward and to the left and was partially hidden behind the beam and the piece of paper, now giving us a reference of distance. The orb was approximately twenty-five feet away from me. It retained the same characteristics as in the first image but with a brighter halo on the periphery.

In the last photo (now that we knew the actual location of the orb), it had moved slightly further away down the hall and was beginning to fade. Dave concluded that the orb captured in the photos was most likely of paranormal origin and was not self-illuminating at a wavelength visible to the human eye. He estimated the orb to be at least five inches in diameter.

As of this date, Dave said, "Those photos were the best proof of actual paranormal orbs I have ever seen." Finding no source of the noise we heard, I felt that the ghostly orb wanted to get our attention.

It wasn't long into my investigative career that I stopped using the flash on my camera for photos. The flash created lens flares and reflections that pretty much made it impossible to decipher anything paranormal. By doing so I captured something pretty amazing one night while investigating in Bellbrook. My friend Jan Berryhill, who was immensely interested in paranormal investigating, joined me. I set up my camcorder on a tripod near the center of a large room and pointed it toward a blank wall, where just a bit of moonlight was able to shine. The room was as dark as we could get it. We used poster board to cover all but one small window, and we taped construction paper over the glass in the door. The camcorder was running in infrared mode.

We were trying to determine what was causing a small shadow to occasionally appear on the wall. A short time later, I became frustrated, stopped what I was doing, and asked Jan, "Do you see something flying around the room?"

"No, like what?"

"Something is flying around us and the camcorder in circles! It is about my eye level and is flying around us counterclockwise."

"No, I don't see a thing," she replied, "but I'm looking at the wall."

What I was seeing was dark. I could not make out a shape, but with the little bit of moonlight, I could see it speedily moving around us in circles. I would point it out as it came around, but Jan never saw it. I took out my pocket digital camera, a Canon Power Shot Elph 110, with the flash turned off. I aimed the camera in front of me at eye level, snapping a photo when I could see the darkness speeding by. I missed it. Nothing but darkness showed up in the viewfinder. I tried it again, this time taking several photos simultaneously. In the third photo, I got it! A white orb, extruding what looked like a blue electromagnetic energy field, lit up in the viewfinder of my camera. It was an orb (really an anomaly) that was self-illuminated, but the color was not visible to our eyes. It is common knowledge that digital cameras contain sensors able to record light further into the near infrared range than the human eye can see. The orb certainly looked like light energy. This was another exceptional catch, and nobody can convince me that it was dust.

The more potential evidence I captured, the more my desire to investigate intensified. The first thing I would do when I arrived at a place of investigation in Bellbrook would be to take photos. I called them "control photos": photos taken on the inside and the outside of the building before the lights were turned off and darkness fell. This allowed me to compare photos taken in the dark, to know what items were hanging on the walls or if a piece of furniture was in the room. In case of a paranormal catch, I always took three photos in a row before moving to the next area. At this time I was pretty much exclusively investigating places within the boundaries of Bellbrook's Old Village. It wasn't long before I noticed a pattern. In my photos, through the viewfinder of my digital camera, I would see clusters of orbs. It would start with one or two, then increase to five to ten, and sometimes more. As I kept snapping, they would taper off, just as they had come. I was curious as to the reason for this phenomenon's continual happening. Were they intelligent? Was their presence simply their way of communicating that yes, indeed, they do exist? Or is the orb a mere conveyance for spirit to get from one place to another?

Not long after this discovery, the Gebhart house came back into play. A young woman with eight kids was applying to rent the house. She was hoping to get government assistance and was awaiting an inspection. Soon after she was granted temporary residence by the owner and moved into the house, neighbors reported that their garages and sheds were being broken into.

A friend of mine who worked with me on particular paranormal investigations lived on the same street, and her garage was also broken into. We had been working together researching orbs. After several experiments using the viewfinders of our cameras, we were coming to the conclusion that certain orbs exhibited intelligence. One night she stepped outside with her digital camera and asked, to whatever or whoever was there, to be shown who was breaking into the garages and sheds on her street. An impressive orb appeared in the first photo she took as she stood in her driveway. Walking to the end of the driveway, she took several photos and found that the orb had moved to the left and headed down the street. She kept taking photos, so she could follow the orb. Approximately four houses down, the orb was spotted across the street, where she photographed it in front of the Gebhart house. She crossed the street and took another photo that showed the orb hovering high over the house. In the next photo it was gone.

My friend and I felt that orb may have been a very helpful spirit leading her to the young woman who was now inhabiting the house and who may have been responsible for the break-ins.

A week later that woman, who was trying to get Section 8 rental housing approval, was found in the bathtub, suffering from an overdose of drugs. She was rushed to the hospital and survived but was no longer able to reside in the house. Once she moved out of the house, the break-ins ceased. I was saddened to learn that a couple years later, she died of a drug overdose.

After conducting two investigations in a 182-year-old farmhouse in St. Marys, Ohio (for a friend and former Bellbrook resident), I concluded that the house was indeed haunted. That was no surprise to the homeowners, who had been experiencing unexplained occurrences for quite some time. They were not afraid; they merely wanted confirmation.

The homeowners believed their house was once used as barracks during the Civil War and that the parlor was a viewing room for the recently departed. During our research a fellow researcher and I discovered two locals who said that the house had been used as a hospital during the war.

The husband heard a female voice speak to him on several occasions while in the parlor, and their daughter heard children laughing when playing in the room.

We gathered many evidence clips, including EVPs (mostly female), constant tapping, knocks, shadows, and several orbs in photos. One impressive event occurred after I had finished using dowsing rods. I laid them on a table with the tips pointing toward a digital EMF meter that we were using, and the temperature on the meter quickly climbed 20 degrees!

Most of the orbs in the photos did not have a reference of distance or intricate features, so we could not deem them paranormal; however, after the investigations, the family noted when they took family photos in the parlor every holiday that there was always an orb or two. The mother emailed the photos for my review.

I suggested that the next time they took holiday photos, they should invite the spirit to please show itself and see if it would do so on command. On the following holiday, they did just that. After taking photos of the children, the husband pointed the camera toward an empty couch and asked for spirit to please show up in the next photo ... and it did. A singular orb appeared as a unique electromagnetic circle of intense blue light energy. A swirling contrail was seen beneath the orb, showing its movement as the photograph was taken. This orb was so bright that I think it was emitting its own light source. Deep down the parents felt that they had experienced a spiritual visitation from the lady of the parlor.

⟿

Simply put, the universe has two basic components: matter and energy. It is filled with jillions of stars and galaxies. Just about everyone that I've talked to agrees that the universe was created. Some feel it is the result of a big bang, some feel a higher power (God) designed it, and others feel a higher power (God) created the universe by initiating the cataclysmic explosion. However it came to be, something infinitely powerful played a role in creating something from nothing. (Many books are available regarding cosmological theory.)

While I do not consider myself an expert in anything in particular, I do agree with Nikola Tesla,[9] who said, "To understand the true nature of the universe, one must think in terms of energy, frequency and vibration." I have discovered that energy seems to vibrate at different levels of dimensional frequency. If the frequency of vibration plays a role in the spiritual realm, I believe orbs (spirit anomalies) need to lower their vibrations to better communicate with us on our level. One of Albert Einstein's stunning insights says, "Energy cannot be created or destroyed, it can only be changed from one form to another."

I've written Einstein's comment in many sympathy

cards, knowing the obvious heartache people are going through and that they may be questioning or searching their own religious or spiritual values.

In my opinion, true paranormal or supernatural/transnormal orbs (anomalies) are transformed energy or pure spirit light forms. When asking actions from them, we must exercise patience. When we ask them to please give us a knock, we need to keep in mind that it may take them a while to lower their vibrations, as they exist on a higher dimensional plane. They must synchronize their frequency with ours to better communicate with us. By the time the investigator hears the knock, (s)he may disregard it, because there was not an immediate response.

My experience with these energy spheres has brought me to the conclusion that they are intelligent and purposeful—possibly ministering spirits.

Notes

1. University of Virginia, School of Medicine, Division of Perceptual Studies. https://med.virginia.edu/perceptual-studies/who-we-are/history-of-dops/

2. Marjorie Hines Woollacott, *The Awakening of a Scientific Mind.* Rowman & Littlefield Publishing Group, Inc.

3. Pim van Lommel, retired cardiologist, author and researcher in the field of near-death studies.

4. Edward F. Kelly, Emily (Williams) Kelly, Adam Crabtree, Alan Gauld, Michael Grosso and Bruce Greyson, *Irreducible Mind.* Rowman & Littlefield Publishing Group, Inc.

5. Edward F. Kelly, Adam Crabtree and Paul Marshall, *Beyond Physicalism.* Rowman & Littlefield Publishing Group, Inc.

6. William James, American philosopher.

7. Alfred N. Whitehead, *The Function of Reason,* Chapter Two (first published before 1923).

8. Thompson House, 24 3rd St., Newport, KY. https://www.thompsonhouysenewport.com

9. Nikola Tesla, https://en.wikipedia.org/wiki/Nikola_Tesla

SIXTEEN

Religious Beliefs and Higher Power: What Is Church?

Many of us were taught early in life to avoid discussing two things: politics and religion. Yet my journey in life, which led me to investigating the spiritual world, has also led me to seek answers about religious beliefs.

What exactly is religion? Depending on what site you end up on when searching the internet, religion is a social-cultural system of designated behaviors and practices, morals, scripture, prophecies, ethics, and organizations that relates humanity to supernatural, transcendental, or spiritual elements, such as the holy spirit (or holy ghost), the rising of Christ, the raising of the dead, and so forth.

But after some lengthy research, it seems there really isn't a definitive definition of religion. The definition of religion is a controversial and complicated subject in religious studies, with scholars failing to agree on one standard answer.

The largest main world religions are Christianity, Islam, Judaism, Hinduism, and Buddhism.

Christianity is divided between Eastern and Western theology. These two divisions include six branches: Catholicism, Protestantism, Eastern Orthodoxy, Anglicanism, Oriental Orthodoxy, and Assyrianism.

Catholicism includes the Roman Catholic Church, Latin Church, and Eastern Catholic Church. They have distinct and separate jurisdictions, while still being in union with Rome. Lutheranism split off from Roman Catholicism during the Protestant Reformation. Protestant denominations include Adventists, Anabaptists, Anglicans, Baptists, Lutherans, Methodists, Pentecostals, and Reformed.

Islam branches, or sects, are Sunni, Shi'ah, and Ahmadiyyah, as well as various subsects. From Judaism stem the branches of Orthodox Judaism, Conservative Judaism, and Reform Judaism. Hinduism is closely related to other Indian religions but can be broken down into four forms: Vaishnavism, Shaivism, Shaktism, and Smartism. Types of Buddhism are Theravada, Mahayana and Tibetan. There are roughly 4,200 religions in the world, out of which Christianity is the world's largest.

Confused yet? There are also agnosticism and atheism, which are not religions.

With various and differing beliefs, one question is still universally asked: "Can all religions be equally true?"

Having had little Christian education throughout most of my life, I consulted a friend on this matter.

She said, "Followers of Christianity pursue the teachings of the Bible. These believers dissect and discuss scripture, and with this a variety of different practices and beliefs follow. This has been found throughout centuries of religion."

For instance, in 1517, when only scholars, including religious scholars, could read, Biblical interpretation in the Catholic Church was given by the Pope and priests. Scholar and theologian Martin Luther[1] challenged the Catholic Church's practices surrounding "indulgences" (the full or partial grant of the remission of the penalties of sin) in his "95 Theses." His sole intention was for his ideas for theological reform to be heard and possibly discussed, but a fierce controversy ensued. Luther and his followers were subsequently excommunicated, which confronted them with finding new ways to live their faith. Because of his steadfastness to challenging interpretations within the Bible, he became known as a reformer, founding Lutheranism (a Protestant denomination); multiple Protestant churches began to emerge.

My friend also pointed out that the practice of religion continues to change. For instance, with immigration, people coming together to worship in the United States adopted English hymns. More modern-day changes with churches continue—for example, churches splitting as some take a more liberal stance, such as allowing female pastors and/or accepting people regardless of sexual orientation.

Religious beliefs don't depend only on empirical

evidence; they are also based on faith. You see, science does not give us indisputable facts. It gives us reason for confidence in an understanding of the world that is developed by careful investigation of reality.[2] According to *The Living Church*, scientists continually test and refine our understanding of the world. "Faith is similar. It is neither blind nor without evidence. Faith is the substance of things hoped for. Faith is the substance of promises that have been made. By faith we hold on to all the promises of God, which are fulfilled in Jesus Christ."

To date I have not found any plausible scientific explanation for God. The sciences, such as biology, physics, and mathematics, help us understand the world, but there is so much more that still remains a mystery.

A presiding priest in California said, "God is not a material reality to be proved or not, but Spirit, a metaphysical reality, and therefore we must learn to feel and live God's existence."[3] Creation itself is proof of God's existence.

⸎

Some will argue religion and spirituality: the similarities and the differences, or how one cannot exist without the other. With a smorgasbord of religions from which to choose, many opt to try to find spirituality without religion. If you ask five hundred people what spirituality is, you may get five hundred different answers; the same is true about religion.

I've heard religion described as a "cozy, warm blanket" that binds us with God. I find it enlightening that we can "choose" a religion. In this day and age, we are free to research, experience, and decide on our own if we want to participate in a particular religion.

I've come to realize there are multiple types of spirituality. Some are grounded in Christian discipleship, and some are not. It is important, if you research a particular religion, to know which spiritual practices are acceptable and which are not.

⁓

Some say the Bible is just a set of rules for Christians to live by, scribed by man. "The Bible is not just a list of do's [sic] and don'ts, nor is it a guidebook with helpful hints on how to live a better life. While it does contain rules and has plenty of guidance on how God wants people to live their lives, ultimately it is a story. It is a great drama written over thousands of years by many different people, but it is one story filled with imperfect broken people, great battles, tragedy, comedy, sacrifice, betrayal, hope, and ultimately grace, love, and redemption to the lost. While this story involves a cast of thousands, the central figure is Jesus Christ."[4]

The teachings of Christ were written down in Hebrew and Greek, and years later translated to other languages by humans. When translating from one language to another, you are also interpreting. Because of this there are some contradictions and flaws; however, scholars believe the Bible is 96 percent reliable.[5]

I've heard religious leaders say that the Gospel (the

four canonical books of the New Testament) is not the law (all of God's commandments), but it is all the promises of scripture. The Bible is considered a direct line of communication from God. The Gospel produces faith, and righteousness comes through faith in Christ. It is the belief of most religions that God and his people speak to us through the Bible.

Most people I've talked to say they believe in God, while others "believe" (but not always in God, as in the Bible). For some, their higher power is nature and the connection that we have with all living things. I define a higher power as something greater than ourselves, and I've discovered for me it is God.

A Pew Research study shows that belief in a higher power or spiritual force is found in every segment of the religiously unaffiliated population, including agnostics and atheists.[6] According to the study, one-third of United States adults polled believe in a higher power of some kind. Eighty percent said they believe in God, with 23 percent (of the 80) believing in a higher power, but not as described in the Bible. Of the 20 percent who answered that they don't believe in God, 9 percent do believe in some higher power or spiritual force. Believers and nonbelievers alike have reported experiencing things unexplainable, giving them all a sense that we truly don't know everything.

What is church? Some explain that to think of the church as a building specifically made to worship in is a misrepresentation of scripture within the Bible. In original Greek writings, "church" means assembly or gathering. Worshipers gathered in the desert, in homes, on the street . . . wherever they could. My friend said, "Church isn't something you visit. It isn't a Wednesday, Saturday or Sunday thing. To me it's God's direction. We choose church and its calling to serve." She continued. "As some pastors may say, we need to be the church."

There are a number of church pastors and faith leaders who agree that we are our own church, and I concur. The church is all about the people, a body of believers with a specific purpose.

The visible church—the actual buildings in which people gather—plays an important role in worship. Most Americans today don't gather in the desert or travel by horse and buggy to someone's home for church. Designated church buildings are needed to host the members who wish to worship together. They provide a neutral gathering place and sometimes serve multiple uses, assisting the community as a whole.

Parishioners of church congregations work together in the main mission of most churches, which is to restore all people to unity with God and each other in Christ. Paranormal investigating and supernatural research, which engaged my system of belief over the past ten years, brought me together with a group of people bound together by a common interest. We've assisted each other in our quest, watched out for one another, and done something together that we believe has made a difference.

I feel that when you shift priorities to embrace your sense of connection beyond the physical experience, it doesn't matter if you are sitting in a church pew or not.

With that being said, I think you should know that as a young woman, I initially had a wonderful experience with organized religion. At the age of twenty-five, I participated in a symbolic cleansing and rebirth by baptism in the Church of the Brethren. My infant son and young daughter were presented to God.

When the "God-sent" pastor of that church moved onward and upward, he was replaced by one who put fear in fellowship for me. After he made several unsolicited and inappropriate visits to my home, I felt that he was overstepping his pastoral boundaries, and I left the church. I didn't make a fuss because I knew that sometimes people may not remember how you came to the church, but they almost always remember how you left. I was on my own and had to find another way, and I eventually did. Through looking for the ghosts, I rediscovered God in myself.

I happened on an article written by Marc A. Eaton, published on the Oxford Academic Sociology of Religion website.[7] His subject was paranormal investigation as a spiritual practice. He said that confidence in organized religion has been declining in the United States over the past forty years; however, this is not to say Americans are abandoning their faith. "At the root of this phenomenon is a shift toward individualized modes of belief and practice . . . identified as a transition from dwelling to seeking," Marc wrote. "In one trend it is referred to as believing without belonging, many people are disengaging from religious institutions while retaining personal religious beliefs."

For the past decade, I was part of this shift. While my paranormal or ghost-hunting experiences helped me become more aware of and grow my spirituality, I found myself once again longing for a collective connection of community. A caring religious community can be an amazing support system.

My one-hundred-one-year-old friend, Jim "Pee Wee" Martin[8], is a former US Army paratrooper who served in the 101st Airborne Division/506th PIR/3rd Battalion/G Company during WWII. He did all of his pre–jump school training at Camp Toccoa in Georgia, making him now prestigiously known as a "Toccoa Original."

Several years ago, during one of my social visits to his house, Jim and I were talking about my paranormal research. He said, "Aw, hell! I don't believe in that stuff. In my opinion, when you're dead, you're dead!"

"Are you sure about that?" I asked.

"Hell, yes, I'm sure."

However, the next time I visited, he handed me one of his WWII books, *Winning Wars Without Heroes*, by Sergeant Tom Adams:[9] a book about his and others' war experiences. The excerpt that he had flagged said this about D-Day:

> Lt. Albert Hassenzahl of C/506th landed above DZ [drop zone] "A" near Ravenoville, France. His stick [fifteen to eighteen paratroopers] was supposed to

land many miles south, on DZ "C," but his pilot had homed on DZ "A" signal. As Lt. Hassenzahl roamed in the darkness he located two enlisted men of his company and they began walking in search of more friendlies.

A lone figure approached them in the darkness, whom they immediately recognized as Lt. Kenneth Beatty. Beatty greeted them and told them not to continue down this road.

"I just came from there, and there's a German machine gun at the next intersection," Beatty told them. He continued in the opposite direction, stating that he was going to "roll up my stick…"

The trio never saw Beatty again. When the company was mostly re-assembled two days later the story about encountering Lt. Beatty on D-Day night was brought up.

"That's impossible—you couldn't have seen him!"

When Hassenzahl asked, "Why do you say that?" he was told that Stick #32 of the 1st Battalion 506th serial was shot down and crashed near Picauville, France. All aboard were killed when the plane crashed, paratroopers and Air Corps crew alike.

Lt. Kenneth Beatty, XO [executive officer] of C/506th, was the jumpmaster aboard that plane. Hassenzahl and the two enlisted men who had recognized and spoken with Lt. Beatty that night (Mike Kriska and Walter Dargis) all survived WWII. Each year at postwar reunions they would discuss this ghostly sighting in hushed tones. All three remembered it happening, and they all reassured each other that they had not imagined it. But they also hesitated to repeat the story, even to their fellow Charlie Company troopers, as they might be regarded with disbelief or ridicule.

Somberly Jim relayed that he had forgotten about the episode until our discussion. In a ponderous manner he said, "I wasn't there when they saw and talked with the lieutenant. I have no reason not to believe them."

Deep in thought, Jim continued, "You know, there isn't anybody living in this world, ministers included, who truly know what happens to us when we die. We won't know if there is anything else for sure until we are gone."

I have talked with many people struggling with what to believe (or not). They have trouble coming to terms with what "God" is to them. Most of them believe in the power of prayer, and most believe in ghosts. I've told these people, "If you believe in God, pray to God. If you aren't sure, pray to the divinity you feel inside . . . the higher power that lies within that controls some aspect of your life."

In general, there are no exact rules when it comes to

praying to a higher power. There is no right or wrong prayer, as long as it comes from the heart; however, if you choose to participate in a religion, each one may have guidelines for prayer that they can share with you. For those who pray to the universe, keep in mind that the universe is only a symbol of the completeness of our being.

In Christian circles, humans are thought of as consisting of body, soul, and spirit. I once had an experience while in that twilight state between wakefulness and sleep, finding myself standing in front of the sink, looking into the bathroom mirror. I saw the essence of my soul shining brightly in the mirror. I looked down and saw my body lying on the floor, like discarded clothing in a pile. I knew I wasn't dead. I felt this was a message from God, showing me my true identity and letting me know I was on the right path. This was a very spiritual experience.

After several years of evidence gathering on paranormal investigations, I thought I had coined a phrase: "We are not human beings having a spiritual experience; we are spiritual beings having a human experience." While I came to this conclusion on my own, I happened to Google the phrase and found something similar, with the earliest match having appeared in an advertisement in *Time* magazine in 1988. Hmmm . . . I guess great minds think alike.

Researching beyond the limits of human knowledge about the paranormal has been an interesting journey. I'll never forget a woman in her seventies sitting with me, waiting for her ride, after I gave a presentation to her group about the ghosts of Bellbrook. We were all alone in the room, when she looked at me and said, "You've been through the veil." To pass beyond the veil is to experience some of the mysteries of the next life.

I wasn't startled by her comment. I simply smiled and said, "Yes, I have."

I have discovered that the supernatural and the paranormal are very similar, although one is defined more as a thing and the other as an event. "Supernatural" is basically defined as relating to an order of existence beyond the visible observable universe, relating to God (higher power); and "paranormal" is defined as strange events or abilities that cannot be explained by what scientists know about nature and the world.

It is said that belief in the supernatural (God) requires faith—belief without proof—while the study of the paranormal should be approached from a position of doubt and does not cultivate faith. I must disagree with the last statement. From my experience I've found that spirits and ghosts do play a role in many faith-based organizations,[10] although those beliefs differ from religion to religion. I respectfully disagree with the opinion of an old friend and pastor who believed nothing good could come from ghost hunting . . . yet it has brought me closer to infinite spirit.

I wonder if I mislabeled exactly what it was that I was doing. Could using the term "paranormal" be the cause of some controversy I've experienced with a few Christians and religious leaders? Maybe I was more of a seeker, as Marc Eaton stated in his article. My experiences since my son's death have certainly been supernatural in essence.

Another friend explained that God knows our needs and can influence the visions we see. Early into my paranormal research, I did approach the spiritual world with skepticism, but now it speaks to a realm beyond the capacity of our perception.

I had the courage to take the leap into the unknown. I spent years gathering potential evidence. If I didn't investigate the paranormal, I would not have researched the supernatural. Believing in the afterlife is not a matter of proof; it's a matter of faith ... but to find the faith, I needed the proof.

Notes

1. Martin Luther. https://en.wikipedia.org/wiki/Ninety-five_Theses
2. *The Living Church*, Anglicans Believe Pamphlet Series.
3. Father Stephen R. Karcher, priest, Nevada.
4. Father Benjamin T. S. Phillips, rector of St. George's Episcopal Church, Dayton, Ohio, "What We Believe: The Bible." https://stgeorgesdayton.org/about-us/what-we-believe/
5. Daniel B. Wallace, Center for the Study of the New Testament Manuscripts.
6. Yonat Shimron, *Most Americans believe, but not always in the God of the Bible.* Includes the PEW Research Center data.
7. Marc A. Eaton, "Give us a Sign of Your Presence." https://academic.oup.com/socrel/article/76/4/389/2461450?login=true
8. https://www.facebook.com/people/Jim-Pee-Wee-Martin-G506/100044537315053/
9. Sgt. Tom Adams, *Winning Wars Without Heroes.*
10. *Herald Journal News*, "What Religions Believe about Ghosts." https://www.hjnews.com/allaccess/what-religions-believe-about-ghosts/article_850d08a4-4320-11e3-b610-001a4bcf887a.html

YES, IT IS TRUE

SEVENTEEN

Divine Affirmation

Life in itself is a journey. This pilgrimage, now going on over a decade, has greatly helped me be more at peace with myself and has made me a more virtuous human being. I wasn't searching for the meaning of life; I was looking for proof that there is life after death. What used to frighten me now comforts.

These experiences reaffirmed that I was seeing what I wasn't so sure I should believe. The insights I gained taught me that everything in life is spiritual, but most of all, they helped me understand that our souls survive death, which ultimately helped me to survive the death of my own son.

Through this journey I was able to rise above my grief, transcending my heart from sorrow to hope, and look for the signs I knew Danny would be leaving for me. The morning after his death, his son was busying himself with LEGO blocks on the table by the picture window that overlooked the backyard. Two birdfeeders hung from shepherd hooks near the back fence, not far below where the utility lines ran. My grandson happened to look out the window and said, "Look at that big bird, Grandma."

There, sitting high on one of the wires, was a hawk. It was not out of the ordinary for us to see a hawk perched near our birdfeeders, but something was different this time. The hawk was much larger than those that occasionally visited our yard. This raptor had a very broad body, and at first I thought it was a small eagle. What I found strange was that the hawk wasn't focusing on the birdfeeders at all; it seemed to be intensely staring directly into the living room window.

Birds are very powerful messengers. I heard that the symbolism of the hawk was associated with light, power, watchfulness, and the heavens. I stared at it for almost five minutes; it barely ruffled a feather. I finally broke the gaze. I did not feel that Danny was the hawk, but that the hawk represented a focused vision telling me to keep my eyes open and my awareness high.

The next day I walked into my office, and just as I was passing my bookcase, a book fell off the upper shelf, where I kept books about the paranormal. I caught it, and the pages fell open to a chapter titled (in bold) "We Are Always with You."

I prepared for Christmas, even though my heart wasn't in it. I went through the motions for the sake of the grandchildren. On December 23, a cold and snowy day, I was alone in the house. I was upstairs on my computer, writing my son's eulogy, when the doorbell rang. Not expecting any more gift packages, I ran downstairs, thinking it was a visitor stopping by to pay their respects. I opened the door and found no one. An icy wind was blowing as I stepped outside to see who could have rung the doorbell. Living on a dead-end street, I could see if anybody had just left the driveway and headed down the street—no one. Hurriedly I ran down the walk to look in the driveway, to see if a car was parked in front of the garage—no one. The neighbors' homes were all locked up tight, with not a person in sight. Then it dawned on me: Danny was a prankster, and my son loved the "ding-dong ditch" prank. I mustered a quick laugh as I went back into the house, remembering a time when he had wired the front door with firecrackers, rung the bell, and run!

Christmas Day was upon us just seven days after my son's death. The first Christmas without a loved one is hard, and participating in a season of celebration so soon . . . well, there was no joy to be found while our grief was so raw. My heart ached as we loaded the car with gifts and grandkids, heading to my daughter's house, leaving Danny's wrapped presents under the tree.

My son's children were spending the night with us, and as we returned to our empty house, my husband went to the backyard to fill the birdfeeders. My grandson and I went upstairs. He walked into the bathroom, and I stood in the doorway of my office, looking for a battery for his new toy. When my granddaughter came to the top of the stairs, and just as my grandson stepped out of the bathroom, the door to the master bedroom forcefully swung closed . . . and latched!

The grandkids were startled and scared; my grand-daughter leaned against the wall, her back sliding down until she was sitting on the floor in disbelief. I was amazed and immediately went to open the door, knowing full well we would not find anybody on the other side. I opened the door, as natural curiosity would have us do, and I smiled and said to Danny, "Do it again!" The grandkids ran down-stairs, waiting for Grandpa to come inside, to tell him what had just happened.

I recalled a conversation I'd had with Danny a year ear-lier, when I came home from a paranormal investigation. "Did you have fun?" he asked.

"I sure did," I said.

"Did anything happen?"

"Well, a closet door seemed to open about an inch, but I sure would like to see a door close all by itself."

"Oh, Mom! I sure wouldn't; that would be scary!"

I had just laughed and said, "I think it would be cool."

We had three days after Christmas to finish prepar-ing for Danny's funeral. I existed in that gap between desire and reality. Heading to the laundry room, as I had done many times since his death, I noticed a neon-green index card sticking out of the bottom of the laundry chute closet door. The laundry chute had been abandoned years before, when I grew tired of using a coat hanger to pull out blue jeans that constantly got stuck inside. The chute had become entertainment for the grandkids, as they would yell to one another from each end and send toys and cray-ons sliding down. I grabbed the card and was amazed to read the words, "BOO! I'm a ghost!"

The handwriting was one of my grandkids', and I figured it was from the days when they role played an animated video game based on spooky events and scared each other. The card was surely thrown down the chute and left there among the blocks, crayons, and other small toys. The laundry chute had not been played with for months. How did the card suddenly slip halfway under the closed door for me to find?

On the evening before the funeral, everything was as ready as it could be, with the exception of finding certain youthful photos of my son. In the eulogy I specifically mentioned those photos. I knew I was missing a shoebox full of childhood photos of both of my children. I had searched for days to no avail. The photo boards that were ready would have to do.

My husband was already in bed, and I went downstairs to the laundry room to bring up the outfit I had chosen to wear the next day. I hung the outfit in my closet and decided to go into my office to check email one more time before going to sleep. As I entered my office, there in the pathway sat the shoebox of missing photos! I knew they had not been there before, as I would have tripped over the box. Just as I had remembered it, tied with a broken rubber band and covered in dust, inside were the photos I so desperately wanted to display at Danny's funeral.

I immediately headed to the nearest store to purchase additional foam boards and began sorting through the photos, having my private celebration of Danny's life as I created the remembrance collage of his younger years.

I made it through the funeral in a bit of a haze. It was

quite comforting to see how many people came to pay their respects. Representatives from the city of Bellbrook, the school district, many former fellow employees, relatives, and a host of friends waited in the long line to share a few words of condolence.

After the wake, which was held at the funeral home, I was saying my last farewell to my son and giving my granddaughter permission to take home the casket flowers that she wanted to arrange in bouquets to dry. My husband walked my friend and fellow paranormal investigator Garry Fox to our car to return his slow cooker and containers after he had generously delivered a home-cooked meal to our house. As they approached Garry's car with the cookware, Garry unlocked the doors with his key fob, only for them to immediately lock again. He unlocked the doors two more times with the same result. He laughed and told Danny to please stop it so he could get in the car.

Not long after the funeral, Danny came to me in a visitation dream. You may wonder how I know it was truly a visitation dream. One reason is that through my paranormal research, I had experienced communication with those no longer existing in our earthly reality. Another reason is that the dream felt incredibly vivid and real, so much so that I sat up in bed breathless, with a feeling of extreme happiness. That dream happened seven years ago, and I still remember the visitation as if it just occurred.

I believe these types of visitations can happen more easily when we are sleeping, while our guard is down.

Rational thoughts are not engaged, and we are more apt to believe what we are seeing (or dreaming).

My dream was in black and white. I had woken up and was standing at the top of the stairs of our trilevel house. There, on the landing between the lower and upper levels, was Danny. He was kneeling on the bottom step, looking up at me. While he said nothing, he had the most heart-warming smile on his face and was as handsome as I remembered. He seemed healthy and happy. He had hold of the top of two large, empty woven baskets, like huge Easter baskets without handles. They were large enough for a person to fit inside.

As he lovingly gazed at me, I felt that he had a great sense of excitement. He headed downstairs to the lower level, pulling the baskets behind him. Just as I lost sight of him, he suddenly peeked around the corner with an inquisitive look, beckoning me to follow.

I descended the stairs, anxious to see what Danny had in store for me. As I stepped into the family room, where Danny, as an adult, had made the area into more of a studio apartment, I was shocked to see the room completely empty of all his furniture and belongings. One of the large, empty baskets sat in the middle of the room. Danny was gone. This was such a shock that I woke up and sat on the bed, reliving every detail of the dream.

I believe the dream was about Danny letting me know that he was truly happy. The baskets represented a rebirth—one for him and one for me in the future. The empty room was him showing me that he was finished with all of his earthly possessions. It was a strong message about new beginnings.

A few days later, my enthusiastic feeling of elation began to fade. I was once again feeling overwhelmed, reeling back into my reality of grief.

My friend Susan stopped by for a visit. I welcomed the distraction from the emotional ride I was on. Although I was functioning normally, I felt like an incorporeal being. Still in a state of shock and dismay, I was sitting on the recliner in the living room when she asked, "Do you think Danny is here right now?"

At that exact moment, I felt what I can only describe as divine love. It was like a euphoric, spiritual feeling of intense joy that drew me into the highest state of consciousness that I have ever experienced. I felt close to God himself. My son had just died, yet I was imbued with absolute happiness. I saw what resembled a white tulle veil gently wrapping around me from a distance. At the bottom of each layer of the illuminating, sheer wrap was a white anomaly circling around me counterclockwise, as if closing the circle of human life. I yearned to forever bask in that sacred and heavenly feeling of spiritual enlightenment. I found myself rising from the chair in which I was sitting, smiling, raising my right hand above my head, ready to continue on my way to what I believed would be a divine union with God . . . when suddenly it was over.

Feeling spiritually regenerated, I realized that my experience had lasted only a few seconds. If this feeling of love beyond description is truly what we feel when we die, nobody would want to stay here in this earthly existence. I believe if I had encountered this blessing any longer than those few seconds, I would not physically be here now. This unearthly gift, again, confirmed for me that there is life after death. While loss is a part of love that we are never prepared for, nothing can compare to the glory and pure delight of eternal life and happiness.

Throughout this journey so many magnificent things have occurred. I can't explain them all, but I'll be forever grateful that God sent me the ghosts.

Epilogue

The little girl Danny loved as his own took on the adult world earlier than most. She has become a well-rounded and self-sufficient young woman, in spite of it all. Her slender loveliness stands five feet seven inches; her exceedingly long hair cascades down her back, stopping at her hips. Her year-round lightly bronzed skin strikingly contrasts her soft, blue eyes. But there is fire in her belly, and you don't dare cross this young woman. She didn't let the world break her, and she won't be taken advantage of. This strong, passionate young lady's weakness is that she misses her father every day, although she says thinking of him gives her strength.

Danny's son is now grown. The boy who once had to look up at me now stands over six feet tall. Within a few years his pants size went from a 12 husky to a men's 42. His height, weight, and shoe size have surpassed my husband's. He enjoys being with family, loves the outdoors, and is generous to a fault. The death of my son was difficult for us all, but this young man chose to cope with the death of his dad quietly. He treasures some of his father's belongings, now precious gifts of remembrance.

Two years after my son's death, my daughter, Jennifer (Danny's sister), gave birth to her third child, another daughter. Courtney Dannyelle—her middle name given in memory of her Uncle Danny—is now six years old. Since the age of two, she was drawn to the photo of her uncle that sits on my end table in the living room, pointing and saying, "Uncle Danny!" every time she saw it.

When she was three, I found her lying on my couch, his photo in her hands, kissing the snapshot. I asked her, "What are you doing?"

She said, "I talkin' to Uncle Danny. I love him."

My son was cremated, and his ashes were spread on the family farm: fifty-five acres now used as hayfields, the rest as recreational land. Danny spent many years on the farm with his friends and family camping, boating, and setting off fireworks. Almost a year after his death, we planted a tree in his memory, about two hundred feet from the old railroad trestle, on the side of the lane across from the lower hayfield. When my husband and I go to the farm to mow, the first thing I do is to ensure that the area under Danny's tree is weed-free and freshly mulched. I enjoy the realm of tranquility as I work on the land.

The summer after the third anniversary of my son's death, my husband and I drove to the farm, as we do every week, to mow. As usually happens, some kind of maintenance needed to be performed before mowing could commence. I loaded the golf cart with my tools and mulch and left my husband in the barn not far from the road, heading down to the lower fields near the river. I was totally alone. I dug a few dandelions and other weeds from around the edge of the tree, spread some preemergent, and topped it with a layer of fresh mulch. It was midmorning, and the dew was still wet on the grass. The fescue, purple field thistle, and alfalfa in the field were about twenty inches high.

As I do every time I am at the farm, I was thinking about my son, missing him and telling him how his children were doing. This time was different. My husband was not with me, doing the usual mowing. I had been totally alone and still was, but I felt a presence. At that moment something told me to stop what I was doing and turn around. I did just that; I dropped my shovel, took off my work gloves, and turned around.

I gazed across the large hayfield. The sun was shining bright, and a gentle breeze was blowing. As I stood there in nature's silence, suddenly—and all at once—hundreds and hundreds of white, yellow, and orange butterflies slowly rose from the field. They hovered as a mass above the growth for a few seconds before scattering. It was a striking occurrence of synchronicity, and I was, again, overwhelmed by the presence of something significantly powerful. This amazing observation touched my heart deeply.

Since the death of my son, I've found the strength to move forward with my life, feeling drawn back to the church. I've tried hard not to confuse my beliefs for faith, but confusing it has been. Religion and church have evolved in the forty years that I've been away, and the "Hell is hot, and sin is your ticket in" philosophy is pretty much nonexistent these days. Some people tried to tell me that my ghost-hunting endeavors were against God's word. I struggled with this idea, as I felt close to God himself. A retired Episcopal priest helped to put things in perspective for me. He said, "What you describe as ghost hunting sounds more like a longing for connection with those you love but see no longer. More than looking for ghosts, you're aware of missing people and relationships with them. The term (for religious leaders) can be a stumbling block, when you try to describe the endeavor."

He continued, "I can't imagine the pain of losing a child. That loss is always out of order. Grief is a challenge, and grieving the loss of a child is even more complicated. There is no timeline for it."

The priest then explained that Christian spirituality around the world has long expressed the idea of "thin spaces," where the veil between the physical world that you can see, touch, and smell is "thin" and an awareness of God's breadth of presence is close. "That awareness comes easily for some people—others, not so much," he said.

My experiences, along with the words from the priest, offered a spiritual liberation that helped me want to renew my faith. I'll admit I'm a work in progress, but my path is clear. I found what I was seeking, thanks to God, the ghosts, and a priest whom I just happened to meet.

About the Author

Marcia J. Treadway is a retired journalist who has interviewed and written numerous feature articles on people living in Bellbrook and Sugarcreek Township, Ohio, for a national newspaper. One story she wrote featured Jim "Pee Wee" Martin, a former US Army paratrooper who served in the 101st Airborne Division/506th PIR/3rd Battalion/G Company during World War II. Marcia also facilitated Jim's participation and appearance (at the age of ninety-nine) in several television and social media public service announcements for the office of Lieutenant Governor Jon Husted of Ohio during the 2020 COVID-19 pandemic.

Her ongoing service to local veterans earned her an induction to the 2022 Class of Distinguished and Honorary Members of the 506th Infantry Regiment (Department of the Army), 101st Airborne Division (Air Assault), at Fort Campbell, Kentucky.

Being away from organized religion for forty years, Marcia has recently joined a faith community. Recognizing her desire for a communal expression of faith, she is now a member of the Episcopal Church. Despite her many afflictions, she lives by the words "Don't define yourself from your tragedy but from your blessings." In essence, she says, "God defines us all."

Made in the USA
Monee, IL
15 August 2022

11714939R00146